MW01533566

Crete Travel Guide 2025

Explore the ancient ruins, stunning beaches, and vibrant culture of Crete, Greece's largest island

Cathy B. Perry

Copyright © 2025, Cathy B. Perry

Disclaimer

While every effort has been made to ensure the accuracy of the information contained in this guide, the author and publisher assume no responsibility for errors, omissions, or changes in details. The information provided is for general informational purposes only and should not be considered as professional advice. Travelers are encouraged to verify all details with the relevant authorities and service providers before making any travel arrangements.

Table of Contents

Chapter 1. Welcome to Crete

Why should you visit Crete?

Imagine walking upon an island where ancient stories coexist with vibrant contemporary life, where each turn unveils a new wonder, and where the natives welcome you with warm grins and open hearts. Welcome to Crete, Greece's biggest island, which seems like a universe unto itself. Crete is a treasure trove of magnificent scenery, rich history, and cultural traditions, making it an ideal tourist destination.

So why Crete?

Crete provides a varied selection of experiences for all types of travelers. Crete offers something unique for everyone, whether you're a history buff, a nature lover, a gourmet, or just looking for a relaxing vacation. Let's look at some of the reasons why Crete should be at the top of your trip list.

1. The Palace at Knossos

Location: Heraklion, Crete.
Admission costs about €15 for adults, with discounted prices for students and pensioners.
Directions: From Heraklion's city center, take a short bus or taxi ride to Knossos, an archaeological site located about 5 kilometers south.

What to Do: Explore the remains of the old palace, marvel at the paintings, and learn about the Minoan culture.

What to Expect: A fascinating look at one of Europe's ancient civilizations, including complex building and artwork.

What to see: The Throne Room, the Queen's Megaron, and the colorful frescoes depicting Minoan life.

Walking through the Palace of Knossos felt like going back in time. The ruins told tales of ancient nobility, while the colorful paintings brought history to life. Standing in the Throne Room, I could almost see Minoan kings and queens holding court. It was an event that piqued my interest and strengthened my passion for history.

2. Elafonissi Beach.

Location: Southwest Crete.

Prices: Free to access.

Directions: Drive from Chania or take a bus to Elafonisi, which lies about 76 kilometers southwest of Chania.

What to Do: Swim in the crystal-clear seas, relax on the pink sand beach, and discover the small lagoons.

What to Expect: A beautiful beach with pink sand and turquoise waves, ideal for sunbathing and swimming.

What to See: The distinctive pink sand, which is made from crushed shells, and the shallow, warm waters suitable for wading.

Elafonissi Beach stole my breath away with its extraordinary beauty. The pink beach and turquoise waves produced a picture-perfect paradise. I spent the day relaxing on the beach, swimming in the tranquil lagoons, and feeling entirely at ease. It was a lovely retreat from the rush and bustle of everyday life.

3. Rethymnon Old Town.

Location: Rethymnon, Crete.

Prices: Free to wander; different prices for meals and shopping.

Directions: Located in the middle of Rethymnon, it is readily accessible by foot from most of the area's hotels.

What to Do: Walk through the small alleyways, see the Venetian port, and see the Fortezza fortress.

What to Expect: A lovely town with a mix of Venetian and Ottoman architecture, busy marketplaces, and comfortable cafés.

What to See: The gorgeous streets, old buildings, and thriving local culture.

Exploring Rethymnon's Old Town was like walking through a live museum. The little alleyways were full of unexpected discoveries, such as modest stores offering local goods and secret courtyards with blossoming flowers. I had a relaxing lunch by the Venetian port, relishing wonderful seafood while watching the world go by. It was an ideal balance of history, culture, and leisure.

4. Samaria Gorge.

Location: White Mountains, Crete.

Prices: The entrance charge is roughly €5.

Directions: Take a bus from Chania to the entrance of Xyloskalo, situated in the White Mountains.

What to Do: Hike the 16-kilometer trek through the gorge to see the breathtaking natural environment and identify local species.

What to Expect: A tough yet rewarding climb through spectacular scenery including towering cliffs and abundant flora.

What to Look for: The narrowest point, known as the "Iron Gates," as well as the diverse range of flora and animals.

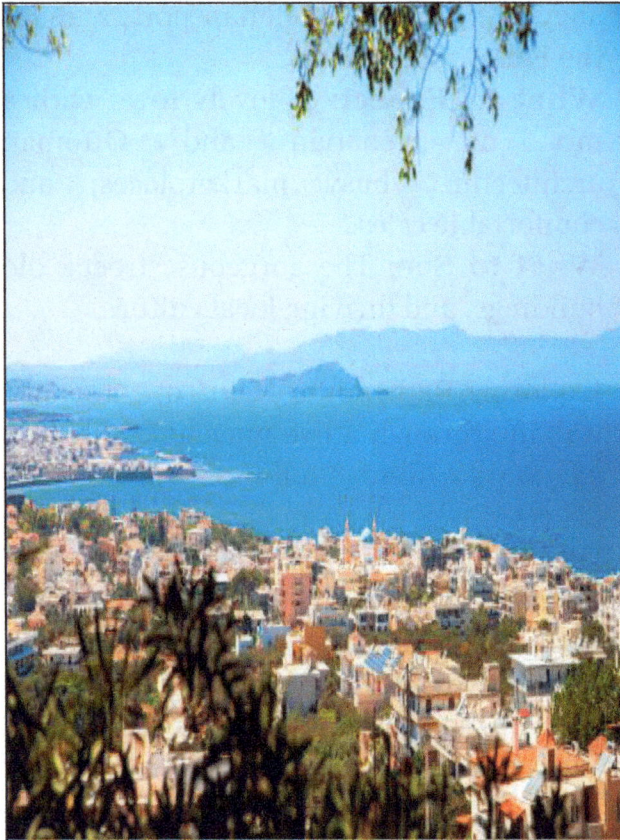

Hiking through Samaria Gorge was an exciting journey. The walk led me through stunning vistas, ranging from steep cliffs to lush meadows. The small "Iron Gates" stretch was both breathtaking and humbling. Along the journey, I met other pleasant hikers and even saw a rare kri-kri goat. It was a voyage that taxed my endurance and provided me with amazing experiences.

5. Cretan cuisine and hospitality.

Location: Throughout Crete.

Prices vary; eating options range from budget-friendly tavernas to luxury eateries.

What to Do: Enjoy classic foods including as dakos, moussaka, and kalitsounia. Learn about Cretan cuisine by visiting local markets and taking culinary workshops.

What to Expect: Delicious, fresh, locally produced cuisine presented with real warmth and welcome.

What to Look for: The use of olive oil, fresh herbs, and seasonal ingredients that distinguish Cretan cuisine.

One of the pleasures of my vacation was the fantastic meals and friendliness. I was invited inside a small taverna, where the proprietor personally suggested food and offered anecdotes about his family's specialties. Each dinner was a celebration of tastes and a tribute to the island's culinary history. The Cretan people's kindness and generosity made every meal experience memorable.

Quick facts About Crete

Crete, the biggest and most populated of the Greek islands, is a place where ancient beliefs blend with lively contemporary life. Crete, located in the southern Aegean Sea, is a mesmerizing combination of natural beauty, history, and cultural appeal. Allow me to take you on a full tour of this wonderful island, explaining why you, my friends, should go on an excursion to explore its charms.

1. Location: Crete is located in the southern Aegean Sea, southeast of mainland Greece. It is the seventh biggest island in the Mediterranean.

2. Size: With an area of around 8,336 square kilometers (3,219 square miles), the island is Greece's biggest.

3. Population: Crete's population is around 634,000, with the majority residing in the main towns of Heraklion, Chania, Rethymnon, and Agios Nikolaos.

4. Climate: Crete has a Mediterranean climate, with somewhat rainy winters and hot, dry summers. The coastal parts are warmer, whilst the highland portions might be colder.

5. Language: Greek is the official language, however English is often spoken, particularly in tourist regions.

6. Currency: The official currency is the Euro (€).

7. Time Zone: Eastern European Time (EET), UTC+2, and Eastern European Summer Time (EEST), UTC+3, during daylight savings time.

Chapter 2. Planning Your Trip

Best Time to Visit

Choosing the right time to visit Crete can make all the difference in your travel experience. This island offers something unique each season, and understanding what to expect will help you plan the perfect trip. Here's a detailed guide to help you decide when to embark on your Cretan adventure, based on what I know and what I've experienced.

1. Spring (March to May)

- **Location**: Throughout Crete
- **Prices**: Moderate, with lower accommodation costs compared to peak season

- **Directions**: Fly into Heraklion or Chania International Airports

What to Do: Explore historical sites, hike through blooming landscapes, and enjoy the mild weather.

What to Expect: Pleasant temperatures ranging from 60°F to 75°F, fewer crowds, and vibrant wildflowers.

What to Observe: The island in full bloom, with colorful flowers and lush greenery.

Visiting Crete in the spring felt like stepping into a painting. The landscapes were adorned with wildflowers, and the air was filled with the fresh scent of blooming plants. Hiking through Samaria Gorge was particularly enchanting, with the gorge's walls covered in vibrant greenery. The mild weather made exploring the historical sites and charming villages a delight.

2. Summer (June to August)

- **Location**: Coastal areas and beaches, major cities
- **Prices**: Higher, as this is peak tourist season; book accommodations in advance
- **Directions**: Fly into Heraklion or Chania International Airports, or take a ferry from mainland Greece

What to Do: Enjoy the pristine beaches, water sports, and lively nightlife.

What to Expect: Hot and dry weather with temperatures ranging from 75°F to 90°F, bustling tourist spots, and vibrant festivals.

What to Observe: The clear turquoise waters, golden sandy beaches, and lively atmosphere.

Summer in Crete is a time of energy and excitement. I spent my days lounging on the stunning beaches of Elafonissi and Balos, where the water was so clear that I could see every detail of the seabed. Evenings were filled with music, dance, and delicious food at local festivals. The warmth of the sun and the joy of the summer celebrations made it a season to remember.

3. Autumn (September to November)

- **Location**: Throughout Crete
- **Prices**: Moderate, with lower prices than peak season and fewer crowds
- **Directions**: Fly into Heraklion or Chania International Airports

What to Do: Explore archaeological sites, hike through scenic landscapes, and experience local harvest festivals.

What to Expect: Mild and pleasant temperatures ranging from 65°F to 80°F, fewer tourists, and beautiful autumn colors.

What to Observe: The changing colors of the foliage, the grape and olive harvests, and the festive atmosphere.

Autumn in Crete offers a perfect balance of mild weather and cultural richness. I visited the Palace of Knossos without the summer crowds, allowing me to fully appreciate its historical significance. The local harvest festivals were a highlight, where I tasted freshly harvested grapes and olives and enjoyed traditional music and dance. The island's landscapes were bathed in warm autumn hues, creating a serene and picturesque setting.

3. Winter (December to February)

- **Location**: Coastal cities and inland villages
- **Prices**: Lower, making it an affordable time to visit
- **Directions**: Fly into Heraklion or Chania International Airports

What to Do: Explore museums, enjoy the local cuisine, and experience the island's winter charm.

What to Expect: Cooler temperatures ranging from 50°F to 65°F, a more relaxed atmosphere, and the opportunity to experience local life.

What to Observe: The quieter streets, the cozy ambiance of tavernas, and the festive holiday decorations.

Visiting Crete in winter offered a different but equally captivating experience. The island was quieter, allowing me to connect more deeply with the local culture. I spent my days exploring the Archaeological Museum of Heraklion, where I delved into Crete's rich history. Evenings were spent in cozy tavernas, enjoying hearty meals and warm conversations with locals. The festive holiday decorations added a touch of magic to the season.

Crete is a destination that offers a unique experience in every season. Whether you prefer the blooming beauty of spring, the lively energy of summer, the rich cultural experiences of autumn, or the cozy charm of winter, there is always something to discover. My friends, as you plan your trip to Crete, consider what each season has to offer and choose the time that resonates most with your travel desires. May your journey be filled with joy, wonder, and unforgettable memories.

Getting There and Getting Around Crete

Reaching Crete and navigating the island are essential parts of planning your

adventure. Crete's well-developed infrastructure makes it accessible and easy to explore, whether you're arriving by air or sea. Let me guide you through the details of getting to Crete and how to travel around the island, enriched with personal experiences and insights to ensure a seamless journey.

1. By Air

Airports: Crete has two main international airports: Heraklion International Airport (HER) and Chania International Airport (CHQ).

1. Heraklion International Airport (HER)

- **Location**: 5 kilometers east of Heraklion city center.

- **Prices**: Varies by airline and season. Expect to pay anywhere from $150 to $600 for round-trip flights from major European cities.
- **Directions**: From the airport, you can take a taxi, bus, or rental car to reach your destination.

What to Do: Upon arrival, you'll find various transportation options, car rental services, and information desks to assist you.

What to Expect: A bustling airport with modern amenities, shops, and cafes.

What to Observe: The friendly staff and efficient services that make your arrival smooth.

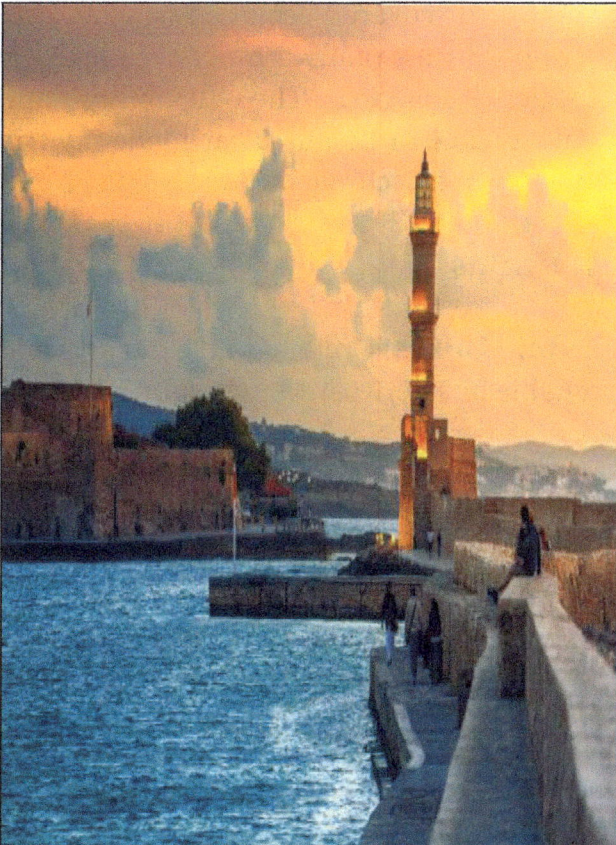

Flying into Heraklion International Airport was a breeze. The moment I stepped off the plane, I was greeted by the warm Cretan air and the welcoming atmosphere of the airport. The process of getting my luggage and finding a taxi was seamless, setting a positive tone for the rest of my trip.

2. Chania International Airport (CHQ)

- **Location**: 14 kilometers east of Chania city center.
- **Prices**: Varies by airline and season. Expect to pay similar prices as Heraklion.
- **Directions**: From the airport, you can take a taxi, bus, or rental car to reach your destination.

What to Do: Utilize the transportation options and car rental services available at the airport.

What to Expect: A smaller but efficient airport with essential amenities and a relaxed atmosphere.

What to Observe: The easy-going nature of the airport and the convenience of navigating it.

Arriving at Chania International Airport felt more relaxed and intimate compared to larger airports. The process was quick, and the staff were incredibly helpful. I picked up my rental car and was on my way to explore the charming city of Chania in no time.

2. By Sea

1. **Ferry Services**: Crete is well-connected by ferry services to mainland Greece and other islands.

1. Ports: Major ports include Heraklion, Chania (Souda), and Rethymnon.

- **Prices**: Ferry prices vary based on the type of ferry and the route. Expect to pay between $50 to $150 for a one-way ticket.
- **Directions**: Ferries to Crete depart from Piraeus (Athens), Thessaloniki, and other Aegean islands.

What to Do: Book your tickets in advance, especially during peak season. Onboard, you can enjoy amenities such as restaurants, lounges, and cabins for overnight journeys.

What to Expect: Comfortable and scenic ferry rides with beautiful views of the Aegean Sea.

What to Observe: The coastline of Crete as you approach, and the bustling activity at the ports.

Taking the ferry from Piraeus to Heraklion was a memorable experience. The journey was smooth, and I spent my time on deck, soaking in the stunning views of the Aegean Sea. As we approached Crete, the sight of the island's rugged coastline filled me with excitement and anticipation for the adventures ahead.

3. By Car

Rental Cars: Renting a car is one of the best ways to explore Crete at your own pace.

- **Prices**: Rental prices range from $20 to $60 per day, depending on the type of car and rental duration.
- **Directions**: Car rental services are available at airports, ports, and major cities.

What to Do: Ensure you have a valid driver's license and understand local driving regulations.

What to Expect: Well-maintained roads and highways, but be prepared for narrow and winding roads in rural areas.

What to Observe: The diverse landscapes, from coastal roads to mountainous terrain.

Renting a car in Crete gave me the freedom to explore hidden gems off the beaten path. Driving along the coastal roads, I discovered secluded beaches and quaint villages that were not accessible by public transport. The flexibility and convenience of having a car made my trip even more enriching.

4. By Bus

Public Buses: Crete has an extensive and reliable bus network operated by KTEL.

- **Prices**: Affordable, with fares ranging from $2 to $15 depending on the distance.
- **Directions**: Buses connect major cities, towns, and tourist attractions. Schedules and routes are available online and at bus stations.

What to Do: Purchase tickets at bus stations or onboard. Be sure to check the timetable in advance.

What to Expect: Clean and comfortable buses with air conditioning and ample seating.

What to Observe: The scenic views from the bus windows as you travel across the island.

Taking the bus from Heraklion to Rethymnon was a pleasant experience. The bus was comfortable, and I enjoyed the scenic ride along the coast. It was a great way to travel between cities without the hassle of driving.

5. By Taxi

Taxis: Taxis are readily available in cities and towns across Crete.

- **Prices**: Fares vary based on distance and time of day. A short ride within a city typically costs around $5 to $10, while longer journeys can range from $20 to $50.
- **Directions**: Taxis can be hailed on the street, booked through apps, or arranged by your hotel.

What to Do: Confirm the fare with the driver before starting the ride. Tipping is appreciated but not mandatory.

What to Expect: Friendly and knowledgeable drivers who can offer insights and recommendations.

What to Observe: The convenience of door-to-door service and the opportunity to chat with local drivers.

Taking a taxi in Crete was always a pleasant experience. The drivers were friendly and often shared fascinating stories about the island. One driver recommended a local taverna that turned out to be a highlight of my trip. The personal touch and convenience made taxis a great option for short trips..

Budgeting and Costs

Traveling to Crete offers a spectrum of experiences, and planning your budget is crucial to make the most of your trip. Whether you're a luxury traveler or on a tight budget, understanding the costs involved will help you enjoy your adventure without any financial surprises. Let me guide you through the detailed aspects of budgeting and costs, filled with personal experiences and insights to help you plan wisely.

1. Flights to Crete

- **Location**: Flights to Heraklion International Airport (HER) or Chania International Airport (CHQ)
- **Prices**: Round-trip flights from major European cities range from $150 to $600, depending on the season and airline.
- **Directions**: Book flights through major airlines or travel websites. Plan ahead to find the best deals.

What to Do: Compare prices, book in advance, and consider flexible dates to secure the best fares.

What to Expect: Prices fluctuate based on demand, time of booking, and season.

What to Observe: Look for special deals and discounts offered by airlines and travel agencies.

I booked my flight to Crete well in advance and managed to snag a great deal. The anticipation of the journey added to my excitement, and knowing I had saved money on airfare allowed me to allocate more funds to experiences and dining.

Dining and Food

1. Fine Dining

- **Location**: High-end restaurants in cities like Chania, Heraklion, and Elounda
- **Prices**: $50 to $150 per meal, depending on the restaurant and menu.
- **Directions**: Make reservations in advance, especially for popular dining spots.

What to Do: Indulge in multi-course meals featuring local and international cuisine.

What to Expect: Gourmet dishes, exquisite presentation, and exceptional service.

What to Observe: The creativity of the chefs and the quality of the ingredients.

Dining at a gourmet restaurant in Chania was a culinary adventure. Each dish was a work of art, and the flavors were out of this world. The impeccable service and elegant ambiance made it a memorable evening.

2. Local Taverns

- **Location**: Throughout Crete, especially in villages and coastal towns
- **Prices**: $10 to $30 per meal, offering traditional Cretan dishes.
- **Directions**: Explore local neighborhoods and ask for recommendations from locals.

What to Do: Try traditional dishes like moussaka, dakos, and fresh seafood.

What to Expect: Authentic flavors, hearty portions, and a warm, welcoming atmosphere.

What to Observe: The use of fresh, local ingredients and genuine hospitality.

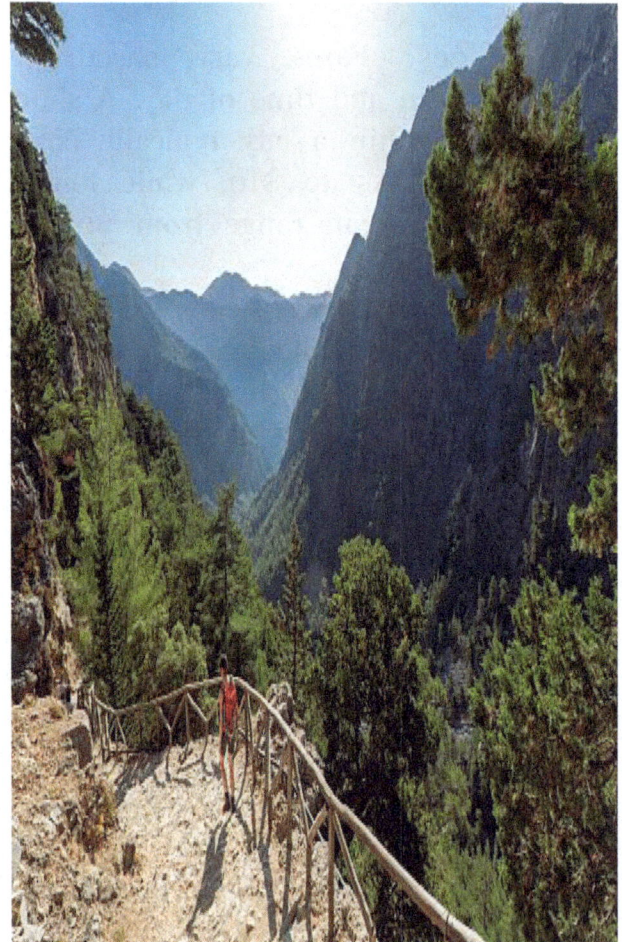

My meals at local tavernas were some of the most enjoyable moments of my trip. The food was delicious, and the atmosphere was always lively and friendly. Sharing stories with the locals over a hearty meal made me feel truly immersed in the Cretan culture.

Activities and Excursions

1. Guided Tours

- **Location**: Throughout Crete, including archaeological sites, natural parks, and cultural centers
- **Prices**: $30 to $100 per person, depending on the tour and duration.
- **Directions**: Book through tour companies, travel agencies, or online platforms.

What to Do: Join guided tours to explore historical sites, hike through gorges, or experience local culture.

What to Expect: In-depth knowledge from expert guides, organized itineraries, and convenient transportation.

What to Observe: The rich history, stunning landscapes, and cultural insights provided by the guides.

Taking a guided tour of the Palace of Knossos was an enlightening experience. The guide's passion and knowledge brought the ancient ruins to life, and I gained a deeper understanding of the Minoan civilization. The tour was well-organized and made exploring the site effortless.

2. Self-Guided Adventures

- **Location**: Various attractions and natural sites across Crete
- **Prices**: Varies, with entrance fees ranging from $5 to $20, and additional costs for transportation and equipment rental.
- **Directions**: Plan your itinerary, rent a car, or use public transport to reach your destinations.

What to Do: Explore beaches, hike trails, visit museums, and discover hidden gems at your own pace.

What to Expect: Flexibility to create your own schedule and explore off-the-beaten-path locations.

What to Observe: The freedom to immerse yourself in the beauty and culture of Crete.

My self-guided adventures in Crete were filled with spontaneous discoveries. Driving along the coast, I stumbled upon a secluded beach where I spent the afternoon swimming and sunbathing. Exploring the island at my own pace allowed me to connect with its natural beauty and cultural richness in a deeply personal way.

Travel Tips and Essentials

When preparing for a trip to Crete, the right tips and essentials can elevate your travel experience from good to unforgettable. From practical advice on what to pack to understanding local customs, here's a comprehensive guide filled with personal insights to ensure your adventure is seamless, enjoyable, and memorable.

1. Clothing and Accessories

- **Location**: Throughout Crete
- **Prices**: Prices vary; local markets and boutiques offer unique items.
- **Directions**: Pack according to the season and planned activities.

What to Do: Bring lightweight clothing for summer, layers for cooler evenings, and comfortable shoes for exploring.

What to Expect: Warm, sunny days and cooler nights, especially in the mountains.

What to Observe: Local fashion tends to be casual but chic. Modest attire is appreciated when visiting religious sites.

Packing for my trip to Crete was an adventure in itself. I made sure to include a mix of beachwear, hiking gear, and casual outfits for town explorations. One evening, as I strolled through the streets of Chania, the light jacket I brought along came in handy against the cool sea breeze.

2. Beachwear and Swim Gear

- **Location**: Coastal areas and beaches
- **Prices**: Affordable options at local shops; high-end brands in larger cities.
- **Directions**: Pack swimsuits, cover-ups, flip-flops, and a beach bag.

What to Do: Bring sunscreen, a hat, and sunglasses to protect yourself from the sun.

What to Expect: Sun-soaked beaches and warm waters.

What to Observe: The vibrant beach culture and the array of water activities available.

Elafonissi Beach was a highlight of my trip. The pink sand and turquoise waters were mesmerizing. Equipped with the right beachwear, I spent the day lounging, swimming, and soaking in the beauty of this idyllic spot.

3. Hiking and Outdoor Gear

- **Location**: Hiking trails, gorges, and nature reserves
- **Prices**: Moderate; quality gear can be found at outdoor shops.
- **Directions**: Bring sturdy hiking boots, a hat, a reusable water bottle, and a backpack.

What to Do: Pack snacks, a first-aid kit, and a map or GPS device.

What to Expect: Diverse landscapes, from rugged gorges to lush valleys.

What to Observe: The natural beauty and sense of adventure as you explore Crete's great outdoors.

Hiking through Samaria Gorge was an exhilarating experience. The trail was challenging, but having the right gear made all the difference. The stunning scenery and the thrill of the hike left me with unforgettable memories.

Health and Safety

1. Health Precautions

- **Location**: Medical centers and pharmacies are available throughout Crete.
- **Prices**: Health services vary in cost; travel insurance is recommended.
- **Directions**: Carry basic first-aid supplies and any necessary medications.

What to Do: Stay hydrated, use sunscreen, and be mindful of local health advisories.

What to Expect: High-quality healthcare services, especially in major cities.

What to Observe: The cleanliness and

well-stocked, and the staff were incredibly helpful, ensuring I had everything needed for a safe trip.

Money and Currency

1. Currency Exchange

- **Location**: Banks, exchange offices, and ATMs are widely available in cities and towns.
- **Prices**: Exchange rates and fees vary; compare options for the best

professionalism of medical facilities.

Having a basic first-aid kit came in handy during a hike when I needed a bandage for a small scrape. The local pharmacies were

deals.

- **Directions**: Exchange a small amount of money before your trip and use ATMs for the best rates.

What to Do: Inform your bank of your travel plans to avoid any issues with your cards.

What to Expect: Convenient access to ATMs and currency exchange services.

What to Observe: The different options for exchanging money and the associated fees.

Using ATMs for currency exchange offered competitive rates. However, I always kept some cash for smaller purchases and tips, especially in remote areas where card payments weren't always accepted.

2. Budgeting

- **Location**: Throughout Crete
- **Prices**: Varies based on your spending habits and preferences.
- **Directions**: Create a budget that includes accommodations, food, activities, transportation, and souvenirs.

What to Do: Track your expenses to stay within your budget.

What to Expect: A mix of affordable and high-end options to suit every traveler.

What to Observe: The importance of balancing splurges with budget-friendly choices.

Creating a budget allowed me to plan more effectively. I allocated funds for special experiences like a gourmet dinner in Chania and budget-friendly options like street food and local markets. This balance allowed me to enjoy the best of both worlds.

Local Etiquette and Customs

1. Cultural Sensitivity

- **Location**: Throughout Crete
- **Prices**: Free, but invaluable in making connections and showing respect.
- **Directions**: Learn basic Greek phrases and understand local customs.

What to Do: Greet people with a friendly "Kalimera" (Good morning) or "Kalispera" (Good evening). Dress modestly in religious sites.

What to Expect: Warm and hospitable locals who appreciate polite behavior.

What to Observe: The importance of greetings and respectful interactions.

Making an effort to speak a few words in Greek always brought a smile to the locals' faces. It opened doors to meaningful interactions and showed my respect for their culture. One memorable moment was when an elderly gentleman at a taverna taught me the proper way to say "Efharisto" (Thank you), leading to a delightful conversation about Cretan traditions.

2. Dining Etiquette

- **Location**: Restaurants, tavernas, and homes throughout Crete
- **Prices**: Prices vary based on the dining establishment.
- **Directions**: Understand local dining customs, such as not rushing

your meal and enjoying the communal aspect of dining.

What to Do: Share dishes, enjoy multiple courses, and savor the experience.

What to Expect: A relaxed and social dining atmosphere.

What to Observe: The importance of food in bringing people together.

Dining in Crete was a leisurely and communal experience. Meals were about more than just eating; they were about connecting with others. Sharing dishes and stories with new friends and locals made every meal special and memorable.

Communication and Connectivity

1. Staying Connected

- **Location**: Throughout Crete, with Wi-Fi available in hotels, cafes, and public areas.
- **Prices**: SIM cards and data plans are affordable, ranging from $10 to $30.
- **Directions**: Purchase a local SIM card or use international roaming.

What to Do: Stay connected with family and friends, and use maps and travel apps for convenience.

What to Expect: Reliable connectivity in most areas, though remote locations may have limited service.

What to Observe: The availability of free Wi-Fi in many establishments.

Buying a local SIM card made it easy to stay connected and navigate the island.

The convenience of having data allowed me to use maps, book reservations, and share my experiences in real-time with loved ones back home.

2. Language Tips

- **Location**: Throughout Crete
- **Prices**: Free; language learning apps can be helpful.
- **Directions**: Learn basic Greek phrases to enhance your interactions with locals.

What to Do: Use apps, phrasebooks, or take a language class before your trip.

What to Expect: Appreciative locals who value your effort to speak their language.

What to Observe: The positive impact of using even a few words in Greek.

Learning basic Greek phrases added a new dimension to my travel experience. The locals appreciated my efforts and often responded with warmth and enthusiasm. It made my interactions more personal and enriching.

Sustainable Travel

1. Eco-Friendly Practices

- **Location**: Throughout Crete
- **Prices**: Varies; many eco-friendly practices are cost-effective.
- **Directions**: Reduce, reuse, and recycle. Support local businesses and choose eco-friendly accommodations.

What to Do: Bring a reusable water bottle, avoid single-use plastics, and respect natural environments.

What to Expect: An increasing focus on sustainability and environmental conservation.

What to Observe: Local initiatives aimed at preserving Crete's natural beauty.

I was impressed by the island's commitment to sustainability. Staying in eco-friendly accommodations and supporting local artisans not only reduced my environmental impact but also enriched my experience. Participating in a beach cleanup was a rewarding way to give back to the island that had given me so much.

Chapter 3. Where to Stay: Accommodations for Every Budget

Luxury Resorts and Boutique Hotels

Crete has a variety of luxury lodgings that appeal to guests seeking comfort, elegance, and customized experiences. Whether you want a peaceful break or a sumptuous retreat, these luxury resorts and boutique hotels provide first-rate facilities, breathtaking vistas, and flawless service. Allow me to take you on a tour through some of the greatest possibilities, along with personal tales and extensive insights to help you choose the ideal stay.

1. Blue Palace is a Luxury Collection Resort and Spa.

Location: Elounda, Crete.

Prices start at $300 per night and vary according on room type and season.

Directions: Approximately an hour's drive from Heraklion International Airport. The resort may organize a private shuttle for you, or rental vehicles are available at the airport.

What to Do: Visit the private beach, unwind in the award-winning spa, and eat at one of the five on-site restaurants.

What to expect: Luxurious lodgings with breathtaking views of the Aegean Sea and the surrounding island of Spinalonga.

What to Look for: The beautiful architecture, infinity pools, and perfect integration of contemporary luxury with Cretan traditions.

My time at the Blue Palace was nothing short of spectacular. Waking up to the sun rising over Spinalonga Island from my own balcony was an experience I will never forget. The resort's spa services, notably the olive oil massage, left me feeling refreshed and delighted. I dined at the on-site restaurant and had the greatest Mediterranean food, with each dish attractively prepared and brimming with flavor.

2. Domes Noruz Chania: Autograph Collection

Location: Chania, Crete.
Prices start at $350 per night and vary according on room type and season.
Directions: About a 30-minute drive from Chania International Airport. Transfers may be arranged via the hotel, and rental vehicles are available at the airport.
What to Do: Relax by the pool, take part in wellness activities, and explore the bustling city of Chania.
What to Expect: A sleek, adults-only resort with a health emphasis, with modern decor and high-end facilities.
What to See: The elegant architecture, magnificent sea vistas, and lively social scene.

Staying at Domes Noruz Chania provided a sense of contemporary luxury. The suites' modern architecture, along with the infinity pool facing the sea, produced a tranquil and refined setting. The hotel's wellness offerings, which included yoga classes and individual fitness instruction, were stimulating. Evenings were spent exploring Chania's lovely streets, complete with bustling cafés and ancient buildings.

3. Daios Cove Luxury Resort & Villas

Location: Agios Nikolaos, Crete.
Prices start at about $400 per night and vary according on hotel type and season.
Directions: About a 50-minute drive from Heraklion International Airport. We can arrange private transports or rental automobiles.
What to Do: Relax in private villas, eat gourmet food, and participate in water sports and activities.
What to Expect: A remote luxury resort that provides solitude, breathtaking vistas, and great service.
What to Look for: The crystal-clear waters of the secluded cove, the sophisticated architecture of the villas, and the attentive service.

My time at Daios Cove seemed like a private heaven. The beautiful property with its own infinity pool provided exceptional solitude and luxury. The mornings started with a leisurely breakfast on the terrace, followed by days of water sports and relaxation on the private beach. The resort's gourmet restaurants served unique and tasty cuisine.

4. Caramel Grecotel Boutique Resort.

Location: Rethymnon, Crete.

Prices start at $250 per night and vary according on room type and season.

Directions: Approximately an hour's drive from Heraklion International Airport. Transfers may be arranged via the resort, and rental vehicles are available at the airport.

What to Do: Relax on the resort's own beach, visit the picturesque town of Rethymnon, and participate in a variety of activities and excursions.

What to Expect: A boutique resort that combines elegance and charm, with individual service and lovely suites.

What to Notice: The wonderfully planted grounds, the sophisticated decor of the suites, and the friendly service.

Caramel Grecotel Boutique Resort won my heart with its combination of elegance and charm. The apartment was tastefully designed, and the view of the gardens and sea was spectacular. The resort's private beach was ideal for a relaxed day by the sea, and its closeness to Rethymnon made it simple to see the town's ancient monuments and colorful markets. The staff's kind demeanor made me feel completely at home.

5. Abaton Island Resort & Spa

Location: Hersonissos, Crete.

Prices start at about $280 per night and vary according on room type and season.

Directions: About a 25-minute drive from Heraklion International Airport. Transfers may be arranged via the resort, and rental vehicles are available at the airport.

What to Do: Relax at the magnificent spa, eat at gourmet restaurants, and enjoy the private beach and pool.

What to Expect: A modern resort that focuses on health and relaxation, with exquisite rooms and high-end facilities.

What to Look for: The contemporary design, the tranquil environment, and the great service.

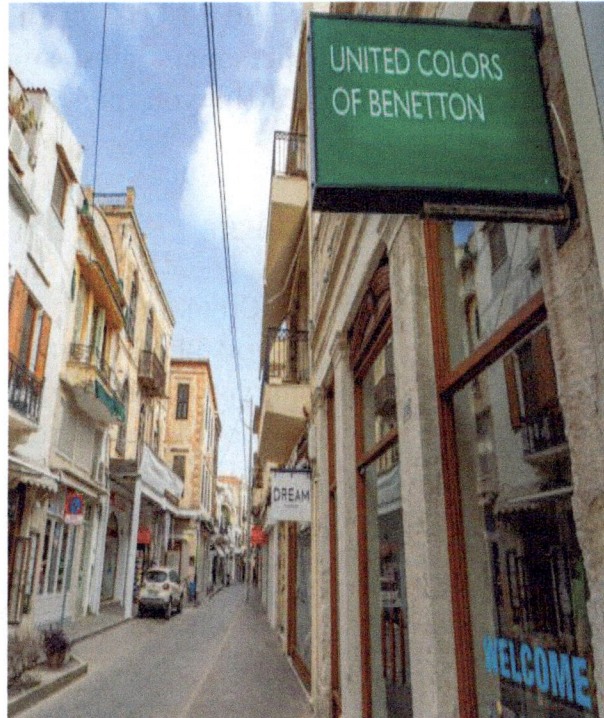

Abaton Island Resort and Spa offered an ideal balance of luxury and tranquillity. The contemporary style of the apartments, along with the quiet ambiance, formed a pleasant refuge. The spa treatments were a standout, providing a variety of revitalizing therapies. Evenings were spent eating exquisite dinners at the resort's restaurants, with each dish demonstrating the chefs' originality and talent.

Family-friendly Hotels & Resorts

Traveling to Crete with family provides a unique chance to make memorable experiences. Finding the proper lodgings for adults and children may considerably improve your holiday experience. Here's an in-depth guide to some of the top family-friendly hotels and resorts on the island, along with personal tales and thorough insights to help you pick the ideal stay.

1. Grecotel Creta Palace

Location: Rethymnon, Crete.
Prices start at about $200 per night and vary according on room type and season.
Directions: About an hour's drive from Heraklion International Airport. Transfers may be arranged via the resort, and rental vehicles are available at the airport.
What to Do: Relax on the private beach, take part in Grecoland Kids Club activities, or visit the Elixir Spa.
What to Expect: A luxurious resort with a wide range of family-friendly features, including several pools, sports facilities, and entertainment choices.
What to Look for: The beautifully designed grounds, the variety of activities for youngsters, and the responsive service.

The whole family enjoyed their stay at Grecotel Creta Palace. The Graceland youngsters Club activities, which included arts and crafts and treasure hunts, were a big hit with the youngsters. Meanwhile, I relaxed in the Elixir Spa. The evenings were spent together touring the beautiful gardens and eating excellent dinners at the resort's restaurants.

2. Out of the Blue Capsis Elite Resort.

Location: Agia Pelagia, Crete.
Prices start at about $220 per night and vary according on room type and season.
Directions: About a 30-minute drive from Heraklion International Airport. Transfers may be arranged via the resort, and rental vehicles are available at the airport.
What to Do: Explore the private beach, visit the water park, and take part in the Capsis Minoan Amusement Park activities.
What to Expect: A huge resort with a wide range of family-friendly activities such as amusement parks, pools, and sports facilities.
What to Look For: The diverse entertainment choices for youngsters, the excellent lodgings, and the interesting activities.

Out of the Blue Capsis Elite Resort offered limitless fun for the children. They adored the water park and the themed Minoan Amusement Park, while I admired the opulent lodgings and picturesque surroundings. The resort's helpful personnel made our stay comfortable and pleasant, providing individual advice and services.

3. Creta Maris Beach Resort

Location: Hersonissos, Crete.

Prices start at around $180 per night and vary depending on the accommodation type and season.

Directions: About a 25-minute drive from Heraklion International Airport. Transfers may be arranged via the resort, and rental vehicles are available at the airport.

What to Do: Relax on the sandy beach, ride the water slides at the Aqua Park, or participate in the kids' club activities.

What to Expect: An all-inclusive resort geared toward families, with many pools, a water park, and a variety of eating choices.

What to Look for: The lively environment, the range of activities for all ages, and the kind service.

Creta Maris Beach Resort was a haven for our family. The kids loved the Aqua Park, and there were enough of food alternatives to suit everyone's interests. The all-inclusive package allowed us to relax and enjoy our time together without worrying about extra fees. The beach was ideal for constructing sandcastles and swimming in the crystal blue seas.

4. Atlantica Sensatori Resort, Crete

Location: Analipsi, Crete.

Prices start at about $240 per night and vary according on hotel type and season.

Directions: About a 20-minute drive from Heraklion International Airport. Transfers may be arranged via the resort, and rental vehicles are available at the airport.

What to Do: Relax on the private beach, engage in children's club activities, and explore the different pools and water attractions.

What to Expect: A beautiful family resort with contemporary facilities, a variety of eating choices, and comprehensive entertainment activities.

What to Look for: The trendy design, the variety of activities for youngsters, and the responsive service.

Atlantica Sensatori Resort Crete provided a combination of luxury and family enjoyment. The kids' club activities were well-organized, keeping the kids entertained while we relaxed by the pool. The resort's contemporary style and facilities created a pleasant and attractive setting throughout our stay. The highlight was a family evening at the beach, watching the sunset and eating a fantastic supper.

Budget-Friendly Accommodation: Hostels, Guesthouses, and Vacation Rentals

Traveling on a budget should not imply sacrificing comfort or pleasure. Crete has a wide range of affordable lodgings to suit lone visitors, couples, and families. Everyone may find something to suit them, from quiet hostels to attractive guesthouses and vacation homes. Here's a comprehensive guide to some of the finest low-cost accommodations on the island, along with personal tales and specific insights to help you make the most of your vacation without breaking the bank.

1. Kumba Hostel

Location: Chania, Crete.
Prices start at about $15 per night for a dormitory bed.
Directions: Located in the center of Chania, about 20 minutes from Chania International Airport. Easy to reach by bus or cab.
What to Do: Discover the colorful city of Chania, explore the neighboring Venetian Harbor, and unwind on the hotel's roof terrace.
What to Expect: A dynamic and sociable environment with clean and comfortable accommodations, such as dormitory beds and private rooms.

What to Look For: The contemporary decor, the welcoming personnel, and the possibility to meet other tourists.

Staying at Kumba Hostel was a really sociable and enjoyable experience. The rooftop patio offered an excellent view of Chania and was the ideal place to rest after a day of exploration. I met people from all around the globe and created friendships, which made my vacation even more unforgettable. The hotel's central position allowed guests to easily explore Chania's picturesque streets and active nightlife.

2. Rethymno Youth Hostel.

Location: Rethymnon, Crete.
Prices start at about $12 per night for a dormitory bed.
Directions: Located in the center of Rethymnon, around an hour's drive from Heraklion International Airport. Easy to reach by bus or cab.
What to Do: Explore the old Old Town, see the Fortezza Castle, and relax on the adjacent beaches.
What to Expect: A pleasant and relaxing environment with simple yet comfortable accommodations, such as dormitory beds and private rooms.
What to Look for: The attractive courtyard, the pleasant and helpful personnel, and the possibility to participate in cultural programs.

The Rethymno Youth Hostel provided an excellent platform for my explorations in Rethymnon. The courtyard was a nice area to unwind and socialize with other tourists. The hostel provided cultural events like traditional Cretan cooking workshops, which enabled me to fully immerse myself in the local culture. The location was great, with easy access to the Old Town and stunning beaches.

3. Cretan Villa Guesthouse

Location: Ierapetra, Crete.
Prices start at about $30 per night for a private room.
Directions: Located in Ierapetra, about 90 minutes from Heraklion International Airport. Transfers may be scheduled, and rental vehicles are available at the airport.
What to Do: Explore the picturesque village of Ierapetra, see the Venetian Fortress, and relax at the adjacent beaches.
What to Expect: A modest and attractive hotel with typical Cretan architecture and friendly staff.
What to Look For: The stunning courtyard, the comfy and tastefully appointed rooms, and the individualized service.

Staying at Cretan Villa Guesthouse was a wonderful experience. The hostel had a warm and inviting environment, and the rooms were attractively designed with typical Cretan themes. The courtyard was a pleasant sanctuary where I could have my morning coffee. The hosts were quite kind and provided excellent advice for touring Ierapetra and its surrounds.

4. Airbnb Vacation Rentals.

Location: Throughout Crete.

Prices vary depending on the kind of lodging and location, but start at about $40 per night for a private apartment.
Directions: Search for holiday homes on Airbnb and choose one depending on your chosen location and price.
What to Do: Enjoy the freedom and comfort of your own room, explore local areas, and live like a local.
What to Expect: A diverse selection of accommodations, from modest apartments to enormous villas, complete with kitchens, Wi-Fi, and private balconies.
What to Look for: The chance to experience local life, the individual touches from the hosts, and the comfort of self-catering.

Booking an Airbnb in Heraklion enabled me to explore the city like a resident. The condo was centrally situated, and the homeowner made fantastic suggestions for meals and sights. Having a kitchen allowed me to create my own meals using fresh goods from the local market. It was a comfy and affordable choice that improved my whole experience.

5. Youth Hostel Plakias

Location: Plakias, Crete.
Prices start at about $10 per night for a dormitory bed.
Directions: Plakias is roughly an hour and a half from Chania International Airport. Accessible by bus or cab.
What to do: Relax on Plakias' magnificent beaches, explore the local gorges, and participate in outdoor sports like hiking and snorkeling.

What to Expect: A relaxed and welcoming environment with simple but clean accommodations, such as dormitory beds and individual rooms.

What to Look for: The beautiful natural surroundings, the kind personnel, and the possibility to meet other nature-loving tourists.

Youth Hostel Plakias was a hidden treasure for outdoor lovers. Plakias community has wonderful beaches and sceneries. The hostel's laid-back attitude made it simple to meet other travelers, and we often planned group hikes and beach trips. It was a low-cost vacation that enabled me to completely appreciate the natural beauty of Crete.

Budget-friendly lodgings in Crete strike the ideal combination between comfort and cost, enabling you to make the most of your trip without overpaying. Every budget-conscious tourist will find something to enjoy, from convivial hostels and attractive guest homes to flexible vacation rentals. As you plan your trip to Crete, consider these amazing low-cost choices that guarantee to improve your experience. May your journey be full with adventure, connection, and wonderful experiences.

I hope this chapter on "Budget-Friendly Stays: Hostels, Guesthouses, and Vacation Rentals" gives your friends a thorough and emotive guide to picking the appropriate lodgings in Crete..

Chapter 4. Culinary Delights: Exploring Cretan Cuisine

Must-Try Dishes: Traditional Cretan Food

Cretan cuisine is a celebration of flavors, traditions, and the island's rich agricultural heritage. Each dish tells a story, offering a taste of the island's culture and history. From hearty stews to fresh salads, here are some must-try traditional Cretan dishes that will tantalize your taste buds. Let me guide you through these culinary delights, enriched with personal anecdotes and detailed insights to help you savor every bite.

1. Dakos (Κρητικός Ντάκος)

- **Location**: Throughout Crete
- **Prices**: Approximately €5-€8 at local tavernas.

- **Directions**: Available at most traditional Cretan tavernas and restaurants.

What to Do: Try this rustic salad made with barley rusk, ripe tomatoes, feta or mizithra cheese, olives, and oregano, all drizzled with extra virgin olive oil.

What to Expect: A refreshing and flavorful dish with a satisfying crunch and a blend of savory and tangy flavors.

What to Observe: The quality of the local ingredients, especially the tomatoes and olive oil, which are key to the dish's flavor.

Dakos quickly became a favorite during my trip. The combination of juicy tomatoes, creamy cheese, and crispy barley rusk was a delightful explosion of flavors and textures. Enjoying Dakos at a seaside taverna in Chania, with the gentle sound of the waves in the background, was an unforgettable experience.

2. Kalitsounia (Καλιτσούνια)

- **Location**: Throughout Crete, especially in rural areas and during festivals.
- **Prices**: Approximately €1-€3 each, depending on the filling and size.
- **Directions**: Look for these delightful pastries at bakeries, markets, and local festivals.

What to Do: Savor these sweet or savory pastries, typically filled with cheese, herbs, or honey. They come in various shapes and are often enjoyed as a snack or dessert.

What to Expect: A flaky, golden pastry with a rich and flavorful filling that melts in your mouth.

What to Observe: The variety of fillings available and the skillful preparation by local bakers.

Trying Kalitsounia at a local festival in Rethymnon was a highlight of my trip. The sweet version, filled with creamy cheese and drizzled with honey, was a heavenly treat. Watching the locals prepare these pastries with such care and tradition added to the charm of the experience.

3. Moussaka (Μουσακάς)

- **Location**: Traditional tavernas and restaurants throughout Crete.

- **Prices**: Approximately €8-€12 per serving.
- **Directions**: Available at most Cretan and Greek restaurants. Look for tavernas that specialize in traditional dishes.

What to Do: Indulge in this classic dish made with layers of eggplant, minced meat, potatoes, and béchamel sauce, baked to perfection.

What to Expect: A rich and hearty dish with a perfect balance of flavors, creamy on top and savory underneath.

What to Observe: The golden, bubbly crust and the aromatic blend of spices and ingredients.

Moussaka was a comfort food that I couldn't resist. The layers of eggplant and minced meat, topped with a creamy béchamel sauce, were incredibly satisfying. Enjoying this dish at a cozy taverna in Heraklion, surrounded by locals and the aroma of traditional Cretan cooking, made it an unforgettable meal.

4. Chochlioi Boubouristi (Χοχλιοί Μπουμπουριστοί)

- **Location**: Throughout Crete, especially in rural areas and mountain villages.
- **Prices**: Approximately €6-€10 per serving.
- **Directions**: Available at traditional tavernas and restaurants specializing in Cretan cuisine.

What to Do: Try this unique dish of fried snails, seasoned with rosemary, vinegar, and coarse salt. It's a local delicacy that offers a taste of Cretan tradition.

What to Expect: A flavorful and slightly chewy dish with a hint of rosemary and tangy vinegar.

What to Observe: The preparation and seasoning, which are crucial to the dish's distinctive flavor.

I was initially hesitant to try Chochlioi Boubouristi, but it turned out to be a delightful surprise. The snails were tender and flavorful, with the rosemary and vinegar adding a unique twist. Sharing this dish with locals at a mountain village taverna made the experience even more special.

5. Sfakiani Pita (Σφακιανή Πίτα)

- **Location**: Sfakia region and throughout Crete.
- **Prices**: Approximately €4-€7 per serving.
- **Directions**: Look for this traditional cheese pie at bakeries and tavernas, especially in the Sfakia region.

What to Do: Enjoy this thin, soft cheese pie, often served with honey. It's a perfect blend of savory and sweet flavors.

What to Expect: A soft and flaky pie with a creamy cheese filling, often enhanced by a drizzle of local honey.

What to Observe: The delicate texture and the combination of savory cheese and sweet honey.

Tasting Sfakianopita in a small village in Sfakia was a memorable experience. The pie was freshly made, and the combination of creamy cheese and sweet honey was divine. The local baker shared stories of how the recipe had been passed down through generations, adding a personal touch to the delightful treat.

Best Restaurants and Tavernas

Crete's culinary scene is a delightful blend of tradition and innovation, where fresh local ingredients and time-honored recipes take center stage. Whether you're dining at an upscale restaurant or a cozy taverna, each meal is a celebration of Cretan culture and hospitality. Here are some of the best restaurants and tavernas that you, my friends, should explore to truly savor the island's flavors. Let me guide you through these culinary gems, enriched with personal anecdotes and detailed insights.

1. Peskesi

- **Location**: Heraklion, Crete
- **Prices**: Approximately €25-€40 per person
- **Directions**: Located in the heart of Heraklion, near the Lion Square. Easily accessible by foot or taxi.

What to Do: Savor traditional Cretan dishes made with organic and locally sourced ingredients. Try their signature dishes like lamb with stamnagathi (wild greens) and slow-cooked pork.

What to Expect: A warm and rustic atmosphere with a focus on farm-to-table dining. The interior is decorated with traditional Cretan elements, creating an inviting ambiance.

What to Observe: The dedication to quality and authenticity in every dish, the friendly and knowledgeable staff, and the creative presentation of the food.

Dining at Peskesi was a feast for both the palate and the soul. The flavors were incredibly rich and true to Cretan tradition. The lamb with stamnagathi was tender and bursting with flavor, and the slow-cooked pork was simply divine. The staff were passionate about their food and shared fascinating stories about the origins of the ingredients. It was a dining experience that truly celebrated Cretan heritage.

2. Tamam

- **Location**: Chania, Crete
- **Prices**: Approximately €20-€35 per person
- **Directions**: Situated in the old Venetian harbor of Chania, easily accessible by foot or taxi.

What to Do: Enjoy a mix of traditional and modern Cretan dishes. Try their famous stuffed vine leaves, seafood risotto, and lamb with rosemary.

What to Expect: A cozy and charming taverna with a picturesque view of the harbor. The ambiance is enhanced by the historic setting and the gentle sea breeze.

What to Observe: The beautifully prepared dishes, the attentive service, and the lively yet relaxed atmosphere.

Tamam quickly became one of my favorite spots in Chania. The stuffed vine leaves were delicate and flavorful, and the seafood risotto was a symphony of fresh, oceanic flavors. The view of the harbor added a romantic touch to the evening, making it a perfect dining experience. The friendly staff made us feel like part of their family, sharing laughter and stories as we enjoyed our meal.

3. Thalassino Ageri

- **Location**: Chania, Crete
- **Prices**: Approximately €30-€50 per person
- **Directions**: Located on the waterfront in the neighborhood of Tabakaria, a short drive from the city center.

What to Do: Indulge in the freshest seafood dishes, including grilled octopus, sea bream, and lobster spaghetti.

What to Expect: A serene seaside taverna with breathtaking views of the Aegean Sea. The setting is perfect for a leisurely meal while watching the sunset.

What to Observe: The exceptional quality of the seafood, the simple yet elegant preparation, and the tranquil ambiance.

Dining at Thalassino Ageri was a highlight of my trip. The grilled octopus was tender and perfectly seasoned, and the lobster spaghetti was a decadent delight. The view of the sun setting over the Aegean Sea was mesmerizing, creating a magical backdrop for our meal. The peaceful atmosphere and the sound of the waves made it an unforgettable dining experience.

4. Avli

- **Location**: Rethymnon, Crete
- **Prices**: Approximately €25-€40 per person
- **Directions**: Located in the heart of Rethymnon's Old Town, easily accessible by foot.

What to Do: Savor innovative Cretan cuisine with a modern twist. Try their seafood dishes, homemade pasta, and gourmet desserts.

What to Expect: An elegant and sophisticated restaurant with a beautiful courtyard setting. The ambiance is enhanced by the blend of traditional and contemporary decor.

What to Observe: The creativity and artistry in each dish, the impeccable service, and the romantic atmosphere.

Avli offered a dining experience that was both sophisticated and intimate. The homemade pasta with fresh seafood was exquisite, and the gourmet desserts were a perfect ending to the meal. The courtyard setting, with its lush greenery and soft lighting, created a romantic ambiance that made the evening truly special. The attention to detail and the passion for food were evident in every aspect of the dining experience.

Food Tours, Cooking Classes, and Local Markets

Exploring Crete's culinary scene goes beyond just dining at restaurants. Engaging in food tours, cooking classes, and visits to local markets offers a deeper connection to the island's rich gastronomic heritage. These experiences allow you to immerse yourself in the culture, learn about traditional cooking methods, and savor the freshest local ingredients. Here's an extensive guide to some of the best food tours, cooking classes, and local markets that you, my friends, should explore. Let me take you on a journey through these culinary adventures, enriched with personal anecdotes and detailed insights.

1. Heraklion Food Tour

- **Location**: Heraklion, Crete
- **Prices**: Approximately €50-€70 per person

- **Directions**: The tour typically starts in the city center, near the Lions Square. Easily accessible by foot or taxi.

What to Do: Join a guided food tour that takes you through the bustling streets of Heraklion. Sample a variety of local delicacies, including dakos, kalitsounia, and Cretan cheeses. Visit traditional bakeries, cheese shops, and local tavernas.

What to Expect: A delicious and informative tour led by knowledgeable guides who share stories about the city's culinary history and culture.

What to Observe: The vibrant food scene, the bustling markets, and the friendly interactions with local vendors.

The Heraklion Food Tour was an unforgettable culinary journey. Our guide was passionate about Cretan food and shared fascinating stories about each dish we tried. One highlight was visiting a traditional bakery where we tasted freshly baked kalitsounia filled with creamy cheese. The flavors were incredible, and the experience of walking through the city's lively streets, discovering hidden culinary gems, made it a truly immersive adventure.

2. Cretan Cooking Class at Vamos Village

- **Location**: Vamos, Apokoronas, Crete
- **Prices**: Approximately €70-€90 per person
- **Directions**: Located in the charming village of Vamos, about a 40-minute drive from Chania.

Transfers can be arranged or rental cars are available at the airport.

What to Do: Participate in a hands-on cooking class where you learn to prepare traditional Cretan dishes using fresh, local ingredients. The class is typically held in a traditional Cretan home or a scenic outdoor setting.

What to Expect: A fun and interactive experience where you get to chop, mix, and cook alongside experienced Cretan cooks. The class usually ends with a shared meal, enjoying the dishes you've prepared.

What to Observe: The traditional cooking methods, the use of fresh herbs and vegetables, and the warm hospitality of the hosts.

The cooking class at Vamos Village was one of the highlights of my trip. Our host welcomed us into her beautiful home and guided us through the preparation of a traditional Cretan meal. We made dishes like moussaka, tzatziki, and Cretan salad, all using fresh ingredients from her garden. The sense of camaraderie and the joy of sharing a meal we had cooked together made it an unforgettable experience. The flavors were even more delicious knowing we had created them ourselves.

3. Chania Food Tour

- **Location**: Chania, Crete
- **Prices**: Approximately €50-€70 per person
- **Directions**: The tour typically starts in the Old Town of Chania. Easily accessible by foot or taxi.

What to Do: Join a guided food tour that takes you through the historic streets of Chania. Sample local specialties such as bougatsa (a sweet or savory pastry), fresh seafood, and Cretan honey. Visit local markets, bakeries, and tavernas.

What to Expect: A flavorful and educational tour led by friendly guides who share insights into Chania's culinary traditions and history.

What to Observe: The charming architecture, the vibrant market stalls, and the warm interactions with local artisans and vendors.

The Chania Food Tour was a delightful exploration of the city's culinary treasures. Our guide introduced us to a variety of local delicacies, each with its own unique story. Tasting bougatsa at a historic bakery was a highlight, with its flaky pastry and creamy filling. The tour provided a deeper understanding of Chania's rich food culture and the passion of its people.

4. Visit to Heraklion Central Market

- **Location**: Heraklion, Crete

- **Prices**: Free to explore; prices for food items vary.
- **Directions**: Located in the heart of Heraklion, near 1866 Street. Easily accessible by foot or taxi.

What to Do: Wander through the bustling market, sampling fresh produce, cheeses, olives, and local delicacies. Engage with local vendors and learn about the island's agricultural heritage.

What to Expect: A sensory feast of sights, sounds, and flavors. The market is lively and vibrant, offering a wide variety of fresh and seasonal products.

What to Observe: The colorful displays of fruits and vegetables, the aroma of herbs and spices, and the friendly banter between vendors and customers.

Visiting Heraklion Central Market was a sensory delight. The vibrant colors of the fresh produce and the aromatic herbs and spices filled the air. I enjoyed sampling Cretan cheeses and olives, and the vendors were eager to share their knowledge and stories. The market offered a true taste of Crete's agricultural bounty and the warmth of its people.

Chapter 5. Ancient Wonders

The Palace of Knossos: A Journey into Minoan Civilization

The Palace of Knossos is not just an archaeological site; it's a journey back in time to one of the earliest civilizations in Europe. Located on the island of Crete, this ancient wonder offers a captivating glimpse into the life and culture of the Minoans, a sophisticated society that thrived around 2000-1400 BCE. Let me take you on an extensive tour of this iconic site, filled with detailed information, personal anecdotes, and insights to help you fully appreciate its significance.

Location and Prices

- **Location**: Heraklion, Crete
- **Prices**: Admission is approximately €15 for adults, with reduced rates for students and seniors. Combined tickets, which include access to the Heraklion Archaeological Museum, are also available.
- **Directions**: From Heraklion city center, take a short bus or taxi ride to the archaeological site of Knossos, which is about 5 kilometers south.

What to Do: Wander through the ruins of the ancient palace, marvel at the frescoes, and learn about the Minoan civilization through guided tours or self-guided exploration.

What to Expect: A fascinating glimpse into one of the oldest civilizations in Europe, with intricate architecture and artwork that reveal the advanced nature of Minoan society.

What to Observe: The Throne Room, the Queen's Megaron, the colorful frescoes depicting scenes of Minoan life, and the central courtyard.

The Throne Room

What to Expect: The Throne Room is one of the most iconic and intriguing parts of the Palace of Knossos. It features a stone throne, flanked by frescoes depicting griffins, mythical creatures that symbolize power and divinity.

What to Observe: The intricate details of the frescoes, the design of the stone throne, and the overall layout of the room, which suggests it was used for ceremonial purposes.

Standing in the Throne Room, I could almost feel the presence of the Minoan rulers. The stone throne, though simple, exuded an air of authority and mystery. The vibrant frescoes of griffins added to the room's enigmatic atmosphere, making me ponder the rituals and decisions that might have taken place there.

The Queen's Megaron

What to Expect: The Queen's Megaron is renowned for its exquisite frescoes, particularly the "Dolphin Fresco," which depicts dolphins swimming gracefully.

What to Observe: The elegance and beauty of the frescoes, the design of the room, which includes a luxurious bathtub, and the insight it provides into the daily life and aesthetic sensibilities of the Minoan elite.

The Queen's Megaron captivated me with its artistic charm. The Dolphin Fresco was a masterpiece of ancient art, and I was struck by the Minoans' appreciation for nature's beauty. The presence of a bathtub indicated a level of sophistication and comfort that was impressive for its time. It was fascinating to think about the daily routines and luxuries enjoyed by the Minoan royalty.

The Central Courtyard

What to Expect: The Central Courtyard is the heart of the palace, where public gatherings, ceremonies, and possibly even bull-leaping events took place.

What to Observe: The spacious layout, the strategic placement of surrounding rooms, and the central role it played in the palace's social and ceremonial life.

Walking through the Central Courtyard, I imagined the vibrant events that once took place there. The wide-open space was perfect for gatherings and performances, and I could almost hear the echoes of ancient celebrations. It was a powerful reminder of the palace's role as a social and cultural hub in Minoan society.

The Frescoes

What to Expect: The frescoes at Knossos are some of the most remarkable artistic treasures from the ancient world. They depict scenes of nature, religious ceremonies, and everyday life, providing a vivid glimpse into Minoan culture.

What to Observe: The use of vibrant colors, the dynamic compositions, and the themes that reflect the Minoans' connection to nature and their religious beliefs.

The frescoes at Knossos were a highlight of my visit. The vivid colors and intricate details brought the ancient scenes to life, allowing me to step into the world of the Minoans. One fresco that particularly stood out was the "Bull-Leaping Fresco," which depicted an athletic and ceremonial event. The artistry and storytelling in these frescoes were truly awe-inspiring.

Guided Tours and Self-Guided Exploration

What to Do: Choose between guided tours, which offer expert insights and historical context, or self-guided exploration, which allows you to explore at your own pace.

What to Expect: Detailed explanations of the site's significance, stories about the Minoan civilization, and the opportunity to ask questions and engage with knowledgeable guides.

What to Observe: The well-preserved ruins, the layout of the palace, and the various artifacts on display.

I opted for a guided tour, and it was an enriching experience. Our guide's passion and knowledge brought the ancient ruins to life, and I gained a deeper understanding of the Minoan civilization. The stories and insights shared during the tour added layers of meaning to what I was seeing, making the visit even more memorable.

Practical Tips for Visiting

Timing: Visit early in the morning or late in the afternoon to avoid the crowds and the midday heat.

Accessibility: Wear comfortable shoes, as there is a fair amount of walking and uneven terrain.

Photography: Bring a camera to capture the stunning frescoes and architectural details, but be mindful of any photography restrictions.

Refreshments: Bring water and snacks, as there are limited facilities within the site.

Visiting early in the morning allowed me to explore the Palace of Knossos with fewer crowds, making the experience more intimate and immersive. The cool morning air added to the enjoyment, and I was able to take my time exploring each corner of this magnificent site.

The Archaeological Museum of Heraklion

The Archaeological Museum of Heraklion is a magnificent repository of Crete's rich history, housing one of the most significant collections of Minoan artifacts in the world. Visiting this museum offers a profound journey through time, revealing the artistic and cultural achievements of the ancient Minoan civilization. Let me guide you through this remarkable museum, enriched with personal anecdotes and detailed insights to help you fully appreciate its treasures.

Location and Prices

- **Location**: Heraklion, Crete
- **Prices**: Admission is approximately €12 for adults, with reduced rates for students and seniors. Combined tickets, which include access to the Palace of Knossos, are also available.
- **Directions**: The museum is centrally located in Heraklion, near Eleftherias Square. It is easily accessible by foot, taxi, or public transport.

What to Do: Explore the museum's extensive collection of artifacts, including frescoes, pottery, sculptures, and jewelry from the Minoan civilization. Take part in guided tours or use audio guides for a more in-depth experience.

What to Expect: A world-class museum showcasing over 5,000 years of Cretan history, from the Neolithic period to the Roman era.

What to Observe: The meticulously preserved artifacts, the detailed information about each exhibit, and the overall layout of the museum, which is designed to offer a chronological journey through Crete's history.

Highlights of the Museum

The Snake Goddess Figurines

What to Expect: The Snake Goddess figurines are among the most iconic artifacts in the museum. These intricately crafted figurines depict a woman holding snakes, symbolizing fertility and religious power.

What to Observe: The delicate craftsmanship, the vibrant colors, and the intricate details of the figurines, which reflect the artistic and religious sensibilities of the Minoans.

Seeing the Snake Goddess figurines up close was a truly awe-inspiring experience. The intricate details and the sense of power emanating from these small statues left a lasting impression on me. It was fascinating to learn about their significance in Minoan religion and the symbolism behind the snakes.

The Bull-Leaping Fresco

What to Expect: The Bull-Leaping Fresco is a vibrant depiction of a daring athletic event where participants leap over bulls. This fresco is a testament to the Minoans' artistic skills and their cultural fascination with bull-leaping.

What to Observe: The dynamic composition, the vivid colors, and the sense of movement captured in the fresco.

The Bull-Leaping Fresco captivated me with its energy and vitality. The scene was so vividly rendered that I could almost feel the tension and excitement of the moment. The fresco offered a glimpse into the athletic prowess and cultural practices of the Minoans, making it one of my favorite exhibits.

The Phaistos Disc

What to Expect: The Phaistos Disc is one of the most enigmatic artifacts in the museum. This clay disc, covered in a spiral of mysterious symbols, remains undeciphered to this day.

What to Observe: The unique symbols, the craftsmanship of the disc, and the theories surrounding its purpose and meaning.

The Phaistos Disc intrigued me with its air of mystery. The undeciphered symbols sparked my imagination, and I found myself pondering the possible messages encoded on the disc. It was a reminder of how much we still have to learn about the ancient world and its mysteries.

The Minoan Jewelry Collection

What to Expect: The museum's collection of Minoan jewelry showcases the exquisite craftsmanship and artistic achievements of the Minoans. The collection includes intricately designed gold pieces, such as necklaces, bracelets, and rings.

What to Observe: The intricate designs, the use of precious metals and gemstones, and the skillful techniques employed by ancient jewelers.

The Minoan jewelry collection left me in awe of the ancient artisans' skills. Each piece was a work of art, showcasing the Minoans' appreciation for beauty and craftsmanship. The intricate designs and the use of vibrant gemstones made the jewelry feel timeless and elegant.

The Frescoes from Knossos

What to Expect: The museum houses several frescoes from the Palace of Knossos, including the famous "Ladies in Blue" and "Prince of the Lilies" frescoes. These frescoes offer a glimpse into the aesthetics and daily life of the Minoan elite.

What to Observe: The vibrant colors, the detailed depictions of figures and scenes, and the artistic techniques used in the frescoes.

The frescoes from Knossos were a highlight of my visit. The "Ladies in Blue" fresco, with its graceful figures and intricate details, transported me to the world of the Minoan elite. The "Prince of the Lilies" fresco, with its regal figure adorned with lilies, was equally captivating. The frescoes provided a vivid and colorful window into Minoan life and culture.

Guided Tours and Audio Guides

What to Do: Opt for guided tours or use audio guides to enhance your museum experience. Guided tours provide expert insights and historical context, while audio guides offer flexibility and detailed information about each exhibit.

What to Expect: Comprehensive explanations of the artifacts, stories about their discovery and significance, and the opportunity to ask questions and engage with knowledgeable guides.

What to Observe: The connections between different exhibits, the historical timeline, and the broader context of Minoan civilization.

I chose to use an audio guide during my visit, and it greatly enriched my experience. The detailed descriptions and stories provided deeper insights into the artifacts and their historical significance. The ability to explore at my own pace allowed me to fully immerse myself in the museum's treasures.

Practical Tips for Visiting

Timing: Visit early in the morning or late in the afternoon to avoid the crowds. The museum is open daily, with extended hours during the summer months.

Accessibility: The museum is wheelchair accessible, with ramps and elevators available. Wear comfortable shoes, as there is a fair amount of walking.

Photography: Photography is allowed in most areas of the museum, but be mindful of any restrictions or guidelines.

Refreshments: The museum has a café where you can enjoy refreshments and take a break during your visit.

Visiting early in the morning allowed me to explore the museum with fewer crowds, making the experience more intimate and enjoyable. Taking breaks at the museum café provided a chance to reflect on what I had seen and to plan the next part of my visit.

Ancient Aptera and Gortyn

Perched on a scenic plateau 200 meters above Souda Bay, Ancient Aptera stands as one of Crete's most significant archaeological sites. Located roughly 15 kilometers from Chania, this ancient city-state offers a mesmerizing journey through history, showcasing Crete's cultural heritage.

Location and Admission

- **Location**: Aptera is located near Chania, on the road toward Rethymno.

- **Admission**: Entry costs around €4 for adults, with discounts available for students and seniors.

How to Get There

Drive from Chania towards Rethymno and follow the signs for the archaeological site. It's well-signposted and easily accessible by car.

Activities: Explore the ancient ruins, including city fortifications, Roman cisterns, and the parliamentary chamber. Take a leisurely stroll around the site to soak in the historical atmosphere.

Expectations: A well-preserved site with ongoing excavations, offering insights into the city's prosperous Hellenistic period.

Observations: The impressive fortification walls, Roman cisterns, and remnants of the ancient city's infrastructure.

Key Features of Ancient Aptera

City Fortifications

Expectations: The fortification walls, extending almost 4 kilometers, reflect Aptera's prosperity during the Hellenistic period.

Observations: The sturdy masonry and strategic wall placement, indicating the city's importance as a commercial hub.

Walking along the fortification walls, I marveled at the craftsmanship of the ancient builders. The sense of history and the stunning views made it truly memorable.

Roman Cisterns

Expectations: The arched Roman cisterns, which supplied water to the city's baths, are a marvel of ancient engineering.

Observations: The well-preserved cisterns and intricate aqueduct system.

Exploring the cisterns, I was amazed by the ancient engineering. The cool, damp environment and echoes of water added to the feeling of stepping back in time.

Parliamentary Chamber

Expectations: The triple-arched arcade building, likely the parliamentary chamber, provides insights into the political life of ancient Aptera.

Observations: The architectural details and building remnants.

Standing in the parliamentary chamber, I envisioned the debates and decisions made here. The historical connection was palpable.

Tips for Visitors

Timing: Visit early in the morning or late in the afternoon to avoid crowds. The site is open daily, with extended hours in summer.

Accessibility: Accessible by car with nearby parking. Wear comfortable shoes for walking.

Photography: Allowed, but follow any guidelines.

Refreshments: No on-site facilities, so bring water and snacks.

Visiting Aptera early in the day provided an intimate and enjoyable experience. The mix of historical significance and natural beauty was unforgettable.

Gortyn: The Heart of Roman Crete

Situated in the fertile Messara Valley, Gortyn was the Roman capital of Crete and one of its most significant cities. This archaeological site presents a rich tapestry of history, spanning from the Minoan period to the Roman era, and features some of Crete's most important monuments.

Location and Admission

Location: Gortyn is in the Messara Valley near the village of Agioi Deka, about 45 kilometers from Heraklion.

Admission: Entry costs around €4 for adults, with discounts for students and seniors.

How to Get There

Drive from Heraklion towards Agioi Deka and follow the signs for the archaeological site. It's well-signposted and easily accessible by car.

Activities: Explore the ruins, including the Odeum, the Great Inscription with the Law Code of Gortyn, and the early Byzantine church of Saint Titus.

Expectations: A well-preserved site with extensive ruins, offering a glimpse into the city's rich history.

Observations: The architectural details, inscriptions, and remnants of the city's infrastructure.

Exploring Rethymnon's Historical Sites

Rethymnon is a beautiful city on the northern coast of Crete, steeped in history and culture. Its charming Old Town, stunning architecture, and rich historical heritage make it a must-visit destination for anyone interested in exploring Crete's past. Let me guide you through some of the most significant historical sites in Rethymnon, enriched with personal anecdotes and detailed insights to help you fully appreciate this captivating city.

The Fortezza of Rethymnon

- **Location**: Rethymnon, Crete

- **Prices**: Admission is approximately €4 for adults, with reduced rates for students and seniors.
- **Directions**: The Fortezza is located on a hill overlooking the Old Town of Rethymnon. It is easily accessible by foot or taxi from the city center.

What to Do: Explore the fortress's impressive walls, bastions, and gates. Take a leisurely walk around the site, enjoying the panoramic views of the city and the sea.

What to Expect: A well-preserved Venetian fortress dating back to the 16th century, offering a fascinating glimpse into Rethymnon's history and strategic importance.

What to Observe: The architectural details of the fortifications, the stunning views, and the remnants of the buildings within the fortress, including the mosque and the church.

Visiting the Fortezza was a highlight of my trip to Rethymnon. Walking along the fortress walls, I was captivated by the breathtaking views of the city and the sea. The sense of history was palpable, and I could almost hear the echoes of the past as I explored the ancient fortifications. The mosque and the church within the fortress added to the site's rich historical tapestry, making it a truly memorable experience.

The Rimondi Fountain

- **Location**: Rethymnon, Crete
- **Prices**: Free to visit
- **Directions**: The Rimondi Fountain is located in the heart of Rethymnon's Old Town, near Platanos Square. It is easily accessible by foot.

What to Do: Admire the intricate design of the fountain and the architectural details. Take a moment to enjoy the peaceful ambiance of the surrounding square.

What to Expect: A beautiful Venetian fountain built in 1626, featuring three lion heads from which water flows into basins below.

What to Observe: The detailed carvings and the inscriptions on the fountain, which reflect the artistic and architectural influences of the Venetian period.

The Rimondi Fountain was a delightful surprise as I wandered through the narrow streets of Rethymnon's Old Town. The elegant design and the soothing sound of the flowing water created a serene atmosphere. It was a perfect spot to take a break and soak in the beauty of the city. The fountain's historical significance and artistic charm made it one of my favorite landmarks in Rethymnon.

The Archaeological Museum of Rethymnon

- **Location:** Rethymnon, Crete
- **Prices**: Admission is approximately €4 for adults, with reduced rates for students and seniors.
- **Directions**: The museum is located near the Fortezza, in the

Old Town of Rethymnon. It is easily accessible by foot or taxi.

What to Do: Explore the museum's collection of artifacts from various periods, including the Neolithic, Minoan, Classical, Hellenistic, and Roman periods. Take a guided tour to gain deeper insights into the exhibits.

What to Expect: A small but fascinating museum showcasing the rich archaeological heritage of Rethymnon and the surrounding region.

What to Observe: The diverse artifacts, including pottery, sculptures, jewelry, and tools, which offer a glimpse into the daily life and culture of ancient Rethymnon.

Visiting the Archaeological Museum of Rethymnon was an enriching experience. The museum's collection provided a comprehensive overview of the region's history, and the artifacts were beautifully displayed. One highlight was a collection of intricately designed pottery from the Minoan period, which showcased the artistic skills of the ancient inhabitants. The museum's knowledgeable staff added depth to the experience by sharing fascinating stories and insights about the exhibits.

The Neratze Mosque and Minaret

- **Location**: Rethymnon, Crete
- **Prices**: Free to visit
- **Directions**: The Neratze Mosque is located in the Old Town of Rethymnon, near Platanos Square. It is easily accessible by foot.

What to Do: Admire the architectural beauty of the mosque and its impressive minaret. Take a moment to appreciate the historical significance of the site.

What to Expect: A former Christian church converted into a mosque during the Ottoman period, featuring a stunning

minaret and beautiful architectural details.

What to Observe: The fusion of architectural styles, reflecting the city's diverse historical influences, and the intricate design of the minaret.

The Neratze Mosque and Minaret stood out as a symbol of Rethymnon's multicultural heritage. The stunning minaret, with its intricate carvings, was a testament to the artistic achievements of the Ottoman period. The mosque's rich history and architectural beauty made it a captivating site to explore. Standing in the courtyard, I felt a deep connection to the city's diverse past and the many cultures that have shaped it.

The Venetian Loggia

- **Location**: Rethymnon, Crete
- **Prices**: Free to visit
- **Directions**: The Venetian Loggia is located in the Old Town of Rethymnon, near the Rimondi Fountain. It is easily accessible by foot.

What to Do: Explore the elegant building and appreciate its architectural beauty. Learn about its historical significance as a gathering place for Venetian nobility.

What to Expect: A well-preserved Renaissance building from the 16th century, featuring elegant arches and columns.

What to Observe: The harmonious design and the historical context of the building, which served as a meeting place for Venetian nobility.

The Venetian Loggia was a charming and elegant site that transported me back to the Renaissance period. The building's graceful arches and columns reflected the artistic sensibilities of the time. Learning about its history as a gathering place for Venetian nobility added to its allure. It was a delightful experience to explore this architectural gem and imagine the vibrant social life of Rethymnon's past.

The Historical and Folklore Museum of Rethymnon

- **Location**: Rethymnon, Crete
- **Prices**: Admission is approximately €3 for adults, with reduced rates for students and seniors.
- **Directions**: The museum is located in the Old Town of Rethymnon, near the Venetian Loggia. It is easily accessible by foot.

What to Do: Discover the museum's collection of traditional Cretan artifacts, including textiles, costumes, tools, and household items. Take a guided tour to gain a deeper understanding of the exhibits.

What to Expect: A charming museum showcasing the rich cultural heritage and traditions of Crete, offering a glimpse into the daily life of the island's inhabitants.

What to Observe: The diverse artifacts, the beautifully restored building, and the insights into Cretan folklore and traditions.

Visiting the Historical and Folklore Museum of Rethymnon was a heartwarming experience. The museum's collection provided a fascinating insight into the island's cultural heritage and traditions. One highlight was the display of traditional Cretan costumes, which showcased the intricate craftsmanship and vibrant colors. The museum's staff were passionate about preserving and sharing the island's history, adding depth to the experience.

Rethymnon is a treasure trove of historical sites, each offering a unique glimpse into the city's rich and diverse past. From the imposing Fortezza to the charming Rimondi Fountain, every corner of the Old Town tells a story of the many cultures and civilizations that have shaped Rethymnon. My friends, as you explore this captivating city, make sure to visit these historical sites and immerse yourself in the beauty and heritage of Rethymnon. May your journey be filled with wonder, discovery, and unforgettable memories.

Chapter 6. Natural Beauty

Famous Beaches: Elafonissi, Balos, and Vai

Crete boasts some of the most stunning beaches in the Mediterranean, each with its own unique charm and allure. Among them, Elafonissi, Balos, and Vai stand out as must-visit destinations for their breathtaking beauty and distinctive features. Let me take you on an extensive tour of these famous beaches, enriched with personal anecdotes and detailed insights to help you fully appreciate their splendor.

1. Elafonissi Beach

- **Location**: Southwestern Crete
- **Prices**: Free to access

- **Directions**: Drive from Chania or take a bus tour to Elafonisi, approximately 76 kilometers southwest of Chania. The drive takes about 1.5 to 2 hours, offering scenic views along the way.

What to Do: Swim in the crystal-clear waters, relax on the pink sand beach, explore the shallow lagoons, and visit the nearby Elafonissi islet.

What to Expect: A stunning beach with pink-hued sand and turquoise waters, perfect for sunbathing, swimming, and wading in the shallow lagoons.

What to Observe: The unique pink sand, which gets its color from crushed shells, the warm and shallow waters ideal for families, and the lush vegetation and sand dunes surrounding the beach.

Elafonissi Beach took my breath away with its surreal beauty. The pink sand and turquoise waters created a picture-perfect paradise. I spent the day lounging on the beach, swimming in the calm lagoons, and feeling utterly at peace. The sight of the sun setting over the horizon, casting a golden glow on the pink sand, was a magical moment that I'll never forget. The beach's natural beauty and tranquility made it a haven for relaxation and reflection.

2. Balos Beach

- **Location**: Northwestern Crete
- **Prices**: Free to access
- **Directions**: Drive to Kissamos and then take a boat from Kissamos port to Balos, or drive to Kaliviani and hike to the beach. The boat ride takes about an hour, while the hike offers stunning views along the way.

What to Do: Swim in the turquoise waters, relax on the white sand beach, explore the shallow lagoon, and hike to the nearby Gramvousa Island.

What to Expect: A breathtaking beach with shallow, warm waters, a white sandy shore, and a striking turquoise lagoon. The beach is surrounded by rugged cliffs and offers panoramic views.

What to Observe: The contrast between the white sand and turquoise waters, the diverse marine life in the lagoon, and the panoramic views from the surrounding cliffs.

Balos Beach was a paradise that seemed almost otherworldly. The journey to the beach, whether by boat or hike, added to the sense of adventure. As I stepped onto the white sand and gazed at the turquoise lagoon, I was struck by the sheer beauty of the landscape. Swimming in the warm, shallow waters and exploring the diverse marine life made the experience even more memorable. The hike to Gramvousa Island, with its stunning views, was the perfect way to end the day.

3. Vai Beach

- **Location**: Northeastern Crete
- **Prices**: Free to access
- **Directions**: Drive from Sitia, approximately 24 kilometers to the north, taking about 30 minutes. There are also buses from Sitia to Vai.

What to Do: Swim in the clear waters, relax on the golden sand beach, explore the Vai Palm Forest, and enjoy water sports such as windsurfing.

What to Expect: A picturesque beach with golden sand, clear blue waters, and the unique Vai Palm Forest, the largest natural palm forest in Europe. The beach offers a tropical ambiance and a range of amenities.

What to Observe: The lush palm trees creating a natural oasis, the crystal-clear waters perfect for swimming, and the vibrant marine life in the area.

Vai Beach felt like a tropical escape in the heart of Crete. The golden sand and clear blue waters were incredibly inviting, but it was the lush palm forest that made the beach truly unique. Walking through the Vai Palm Forest, I felt like I had been transported to an exotic paradise. The beach itself offered a perfect blend of relaxation and adventure, with options for water sports and exploring the vibrant marine life. Watching the sunset over the palm trees and the sea was a sight that will forever be etched in my memory.

Practical Tips for Visiting

Timing: Visit early in the morning or late in the afternoon to avoid the crowds and the midday heat. The best times to visit are during the shoulder seasons (spring and fall) when the weather is pleasant and the beaches are less crowded.

Accessibility: Wear comfortable shoes if you plan to hike to the beaches, and bring water and snacks as facilities may be limited.

Photography: Bring a camera to capture the stunning landscapes, but be mindful of protecting your equipment from sand and water.

Facilities: Some beaches may have limited facilities, so consider bringing essentials such as water, snacks, and sun protection. Check if there are available amenities like restrooms, showers, and beach bars.

Visiting these beaches early in the morning allowed me to enjoy their beauty in peace and solitude. The quiet moments spent walking along the shore and watching the sunrise added to the magic of the experience. Bringing water and snacks ensured that I could spend the whole day exploring without needing to leave for provisions.

Hiking Samaria Gorge: A Trekking Adventure

Samaria Gorge is one of the most spectacular natural wonders of Crete and a paradise for trekking enthusiasts. This stunning gorge, located in the White Mountains, offers an unforgettable hiking adventure through breathtaking landscapes and rich biodiversity. Let me guide you through the experience of hiking Samaria Gorge, filled with personal anecdotes and detailed insights to help you fully appreciate its beauty and challenge.

Location and Prices

- **Location**: White Mountains, Crete
- **Prices**: Entrance fee is approximately €5.
- **Directions**: From Chania, take a bus to the entrance at Xyloskalo, located in the White Mountains. The bus journey takes about 1.5 hours. Alternatively, you can drive to the entrance or join a guided tour that includes transportation.

What to Do: Hike the 16-kilometer trail through the gorge, enjoy the stunning natural scenery, and spot local wildlife.

The hike typically takes 4-7 hours, depending on your pace and fitness level.

What to Expect: A challenging but rewarding hike through one of Europe's longest gorges, featuring dramatic landscapes, towering cliffs, lush vegetation, and a variety of flora and fauna.

What to Observe: The narrowest point, known as the "Iron Gates," the rich biodiversity, including rare species like the kri-kri (Cretan wild goat), and the remnants of ancient settlements.

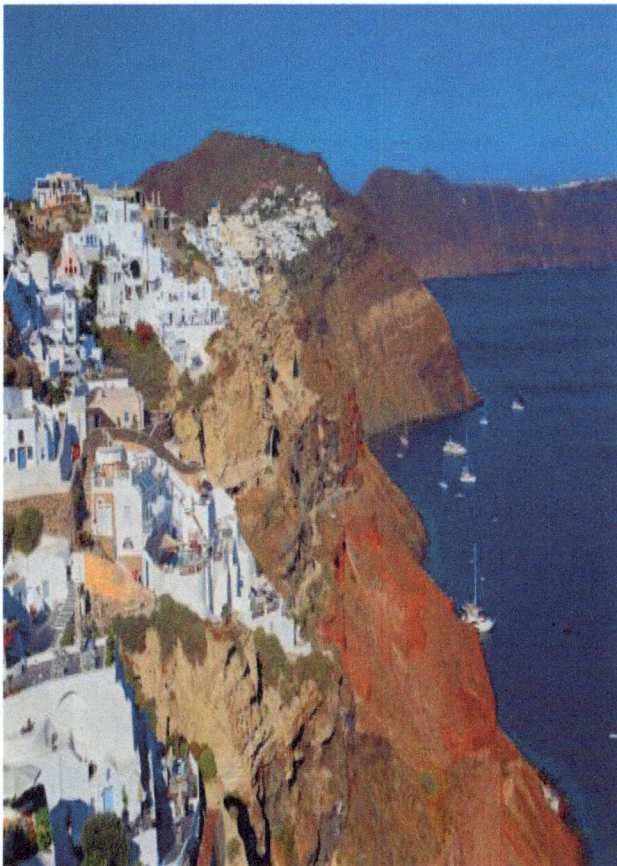

Preparing for the Hike

What to Bring: Wear sturdy hiking boots, bring plenty of water, snacks, a hat, sunscreen, and a first-aid kit. Dress in layers, as the temperature can vary throughout the day.

What to Do: Start early in the morning to avoid the midday heat and ensure you have enough time to complete the hike before dark. Be prepared for a long and strenuous trek with uneven terrain and rocky paths.

What to Expect: A mix of steep descents, narrow passages, and rocky paths. The trail is well-marked, but the terrain can be challenging.

What to Observe: The changing landscapes, from dense forests to rocky cliffs, and the sounds of nature, including birdsong and the gentle flow of the river.

Preparing for the hike was an adventure in itself. I packed my backpack with all the essentials and made sure to wear comfortable hiking boots. The anticipation and excitement of embarking on this epic trek filled me with energy. Starting early in the morning, the cool air and the sound of birdsong created a serene and invigorating atmosphere.

The Hike Begins: Xyloskalo to Agia Roumeli

1. Xyloskalo Entrance

What to Expect: The hike begins at the Xyloskalo entrance, located at an altitude of 1,230 meters. The initial descent is steep, with a series of wooden steps leading down into the gorge.

What to Observe: The breathtaking views of the White Mountains, the lush vegetation, and the crystal-clear river flowing through the gorge.

Standing at the Xyloskalo entrance, I took a deep breath and admired the panoramic views of the White Mountains. The descent was steep, but the excitement of starting the hike made it exhilarating. The wooden steps and the sound of the river below added to the sense of adventure.

2. Iron Gates (Portes)

What to Expect: The narrowest point of the gorge, known as the "Iron Gates" or "Portes," is just 3 meters wide and flanked by towering cliffs reaching up to 300 meters high.

What to Observe: The dramatic rock formations, the narrow passage, and the sense of awe as you pass through this natural marvel.

Reaching the Iron Gates was a moment of awe and wonder. The sheer cliffs towering above and the narrow passage created a sense of intimacy with nature's grandeur. Walking through the Iron Gates, I felt a surge of accomplishment and admiration for the raw beauty of the gorge.

3. Rest Points and Springs

What to Expect: Along the trail, there are several rest points with benches and springs where you can refill your water bottle. These spots offer a chance to rest, hydrate, and enjoy the surrounding scenery.

What to Observe: The clear, cool water from the springs, the shady spots under the trees, and the camaraderie among fellow hikers.

Taking breaks at the rest points was a welcome relief. The clear, refreshing water from the springs was invigorating, and the shady spots provided a perfect place to rest and recharge. Sharing stories and tips with fellow hikers created a sense of camaraderie and community.

4. Ancient Settlements

What to Expect: The trail passes through the remnants of ancient settlements, including the village of Samaria, which was abandoned in 1962. These ruins offer a glimpse into the history and culture of the area.

What to Observe: The stone houses, the old church, and the signs of past human habitation amidst the natural beauty of the gorge.

Exploring the ancient village of Samaria was a poignant experience. The stone houses and the old church, now silent and abandoned, told stories of a once-thriving community. The juxtaposition of human history and natural beauty added depth to the hike.

Exploring Psiloritis Natural Park and the White Mountains

Crete's natural beauty is truly breathtaking, and two of its most captivating landscapes are the Psiloritis Natural Park and the White Mountains. These areas offer unparalleled opportunities for outdoor adventures, from hiking and climbing to exploring unique ecosystems. Let me take you on an extensive journey through these natural wonders, enriched with personal anecdotes and detailed insights to help you fully appreciate their splendor.

1. Psiloritis Natural Park (Mount Ida)

Location and Prices

- **Location**: Central Crete
- **Prices**: Free to access
- **Directions**: The park is located in the central part of Crete, with the easiest access points being from Anogia, Krousonas, and Zaros. You can drive to these villages or take public transportation from major cities like Heraklion and Rethymnon.

What to Do: Hike to the summit of Mount Ida, explore the Idaean Cave (mythologically known as the birthplace of Zeus), and visit the Nida Plateau. Participate in guided tours to learn about the area's rich biodiversity and cultural heritage.

What to Expect: A diverse landscape featuring rugged mountains, fertile plateaus, and lush forests. The park is home to a variety of flora and fauna, as well as significant archaeological sites.

What to Observe: The unique geological formations, endemic plant species, and the stunning panoramic views from the summit of Mount Ida.

Hiking to the summit of Mount Ida was an exhilarating experience. The trail was challenging, but the sense of accomplishment and the breathtaking views from the top made it all worthwhile. The legend of Zeus added a mystical element to the journey, making me feel like I was walking in the footsteps of ancient gods. The Idaean Cave was a fascinating site, with its dark, cool interior and the sense of ancient history that permeated the air.

Hiking to the Summit of Mount Ida

What to Expect: The hike to the summit of Mount Ida (2,456 meters) is a challenging but rewarding trek, offering stunning views of the surrounding landscape.

What to Observe: The changing vegetation as you ascend, from olive groves and vineyards to alpine meadows and rocky terrain. The summit offers panoramic views of Crete and the Aegean Sea.

Reaching the summit of Mount Ida was a moment of pure triumph. The climb was demanding, but the sense of being on top of the world was indescribable. The view stretched endlessly in all directions, with the Aegean Sea glistening in the distance. It was a moment of profound connection with nature and the island's ancient past.

Exploring the Idaean Cave

What to Expect: The Idaean Cave, also known as the birthplace of Zeus, is a significant archaeological and mythological site. The cave is adorned with stalactites and stalagmites and offers a sense of awe and wonder.

What to Observe: The unique rock formations, the cool, dark interior of the cave, and the sense of ancient history and mythology.

Stepping into the Idaean Cave felt like entering another world. The air was cool and still, and the flickering torchlight cast eerie shadows on the rock formations. Knowing that this cave was steeped in mythological significance added to the sense of wonder. It was easy to imagine the ancient rituals that might have taken place here, honoring the god of gods.

Visiting the Nida Plateau

What to Expect: The Nida Plateau is a fertile highland area known for its agricultural activities and traditional shepherding practices. The plateau is surrounded by the rugged peaks of the Psiloritis range.

What to Observe: The lush vegetation, the traditional stone shepherd huts (mitata), and the grazing flocks of sheep and goats.

The Nida Plateau was a serene and picturesque landscape. The sight of the traditional shepherd huts and the grazing animals added a timeless quality to the scene. I spent a peaceful afternoon exploring the plateau, enjoying the fresh mountain air and the sense of tranquility. It was a perfect escape from the hustle and bustle of modern life.

2. The White Mountains (Lefka Ori)

Location and Prices

- **Location**: Western Crete
- **Prices**: Free to access
- **Directions**: The White Mountains are located in western Crete, with access points from Chania, Omalos, and Sfakia. You can drive to these villages or take public transportation from major cities like Chania and Rethymnon.

What to Do: Hike the Samaria Gorge, explore the high-altitude plains of Omalos, and climb the highest peak, Pachnes. Participate in guided tours to learn about the unique ecosystems and geological features of the White Mountains.

What to Expect: A dramatic landscape of rugged peaks, deep gorges, and high-altitude plains. The White Mountains are home to a rich diversity of flora and fauna, including endemic species.

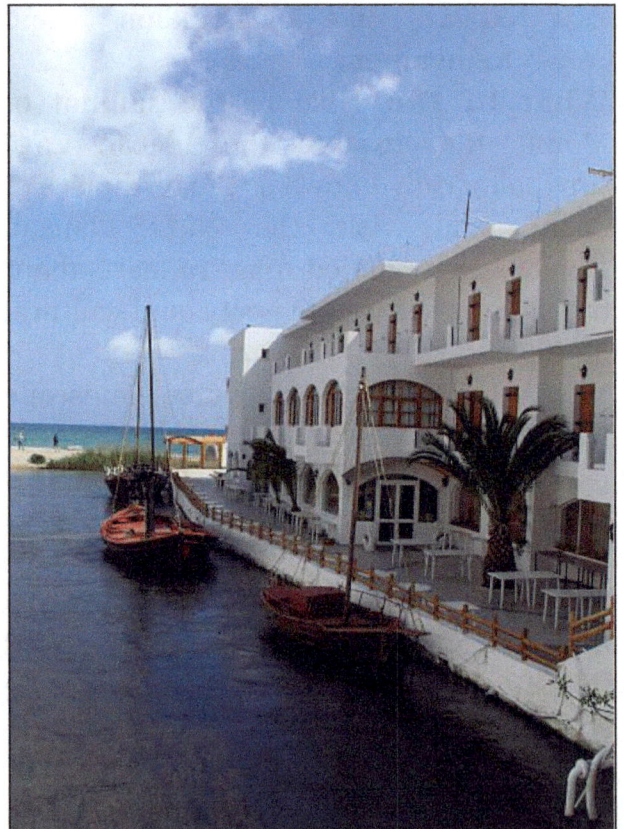

What to Observe: The stark beauty of the limestone peaks, the vibrant wildflowers, and the diverse wildlife, including the rare Cretan wild goat (kri-kri).

The White Mountains were a dramatic and awe-inspiring landscape. The rugged peaks and deep gorges created a sense of adventure and exploration. Climbing the highest peak, Pachnes, was a challenging but exhilarating experience. The view from the top was nothing short of spectacular, with the rugged terrain stretching out below and the sea shimmering in the distance.

Hiking the Samaria Gorge

What to Expect: The Samaria Gorge, one of the longest gorges in Europe, offers a challenging and rewarding hike through stunning natural scenery.

What to Observe: The towering cliffs, the diverse flora and fauna, and the narrow passage known as the "Iron Gates."

Hiking the Samaria Gorge was an unforgettable adventure. The dramatic cliffs and the lush vegetation created a breathtaking backdrop for the trek. The sense of accomplishment at the end of the hike, along with the beauty of the landscape, made it a truly memorable experience.

Exploring the Omalos Plateau

What to Expect: The Omalos Plateau is a high-altitude plain surrounded by the White Mountains, offering a unique landscape of grasslands and traditional agriculture.

What to Observe: The vibrant wildflowers, the traditional stone houses, and the grazing sheep and goats.

The Omalos Plateau was a tranquil and beautiful landscape. The sight of the wildflowers in full bloom and the traditional stone houses added to the charm of the area. It was a perfect place to relax and enjoy the natural beauty of the White Mountains.

Climbing Pachnes

What to Expect: Pachnes, the highest peak in the White Mountains at 2,453 meters, offers a challenging and rewarding climb with stunning panoramic views.

What to Observe: The rugged terrain, the unique rock formations, and the expansive views from the summit.

Climbing Pachnes was a challenging but exhilarating experience. The rugged terrain and the changing landscapes kept the climb interesting, and the view from the summit was absolutely breathtaking. It was a moment of triumph and a deep connection with the natural beauty of Crete.

Practical Tips for Exploring

Timing: Visit during the spring or fall for the best weather and fewer crowds. Summer can be hot, and winter may bring snow to the higher elevations.

Accessibility: Wear sturdy hiking boots, bring plenty of water, snacks, a hat, sunscreen, and a first-aid kit. Dress in layers, as the temperature can vary throughout the day.

Safety: Stay on marked trails, watch your footing, and be mindful of the weather conditions. Carry a first-aid kit and know how to use it.

Photography: Bring a camera to capture the stunning landscapes, but be mindful of protecting your equipment from dust and moisture.

Refreshments: Bring water, snacks, and sun protection. There are limited facilities in some areas, so be prepared with essentials.

Visiting during the spring allowed me to enjoy the beautiful wildflowers in full bloom and the pleasant weather. Staying hydrated and taking breaks to enjoy the scenery made the experience even more enjoyable. The sense of adventure and the connection with nature made every moment memorable.

Hidden Gems: Secluded Beaches and Lesser-Known Trails

Crete's natural beauty is vast and varied, offering hidden gems that provide a more intimate and serene experience away from the bustling crowds. Discovering these secluded beaches and lesser-known trails allows you to connect with the island's pristine landscapes and savor moments of tranquility. Let me guide you through some of these hidden treasures, enriched with personal anecdotes and detailed insights to help you fully appreciate their charm.

Secluded Beaches

1. Seitan Limania Beach

- **Location**: Northeastern coast of the Akrotiri Peninsula, near Chania
- **Prices**: Free to access
- **Directions**: Drive from Chania to the Akrotiri Peninsula, following the signs to Seitan Limania. The drive takes about 30 minutes. A steep, winding path leads down to the beach from the parking area.

What to Do: Swim in the crystal-clear waters, relax on the pebble beach, and enjoy the dramatic cliffs surrounding the cove.

What to Expect: A hidden cove with turquoise waters and a small pebble beach, surrounded by steep cliffs. The beach is secluded and offers a sense of adventure.

What to Observe: The contrast between the turquoise waters and the rugged cliffs, the tranquility of the secluded cove, and the vibrant marine life.

Seitan Limania Beach was a hidden paradise that took my breath away. The drive to the beach was an adventure in itself, with winding roads offering stunning views of the coastline. The steep path down to the beach added to the sense of discovery. Once I reached the cove, the turquoise waters and the dramatic cliffs created a scene of unparalleled beauty. Swimming in the clear waters and lounging on the pebble beach felt like a dream come true.

2. Triopetra Beach

- **Location**: Southern coast of Crete, near Akoumia village
- **Prices**: Free to access
- **Directions**: Drive from Rethymnon to Akoumia village, then follow the signs to Triopetra Beach. The drive takes about 50 minutes.

What to Do: Relax on the golden sand, swim in the clear waters, explore the unique rock formations, and enjoy a meal at the nearby tavernas.

What to Expect: A long stretch of golden sand with crystal-clear waters, flanked by three distinctive rock formations that give the beach its name.

What to Observe: The impressive rock formations, the serene atmosphere, and the stunning sunsets over the Libyan Sea.

Triopetra Beach was a serene escape that offered a perfect blend of natural beauty and tranquility. The three rock formations rising from the sea were a striking sight, adding a unique character to the beach. I spent the day swimming in the clear waters, relaxing on the golden sand, and exploring the rock formations. The highlight was watching the sun set over the Libyan Sea, casting a golden glow on the landscape. It was a moment of pure bliss and connection with nature.

3. Glyka Nera Beach

- **Location**: Southwestern coast of Crete, near Chora Sfakion
- **Prices**: Free to access
- **Directions**: From Chora Sfakion, you can either take a boat or hike to Glyka Nera Beach. The hike takes about 1.5 hours and offers stunning coastal views.

What to Do: Swim in the clear waters, relax on the pebble beach, and enjoy the natural freshwater springs that flow into the sea.

What to Expect: A secluded pebble beach with crystal-clear waters and natural freshwater springs. The beach is accessible by boat or a scenic coastal hike.

What to Observe: The unique combination of freshwater springs and seawater, the tranquil atmosphere, and the dramatic coastal cliffs.

Hiking to Glyka Nera Beach was an adventure filled with breathtaking coastal views. The path hugged the cliffs, offering stunning vistas of the sea below. Reaching the beach, I was greeted by the sight of clear waters and the soothing sound of natural springs. Swimming in the cool, refreshing water and relaxing on the pebble beach was a rejuvenating experience. The sense of seclusion and the natural beauty of Glyka Nera made it a hidden gem worth discovering.

Lesser-Known Trails

1. Rouvas Gorge Trail

- **Location**: Central Crete, near Zaros village
- **Prices**: Free to access
- **Directions**: Drive to Zaros village, then follow the signs to Rouvas Gorge. The hike begins at Lake Zaros and follows the river upstream.

What to Do: Hike through the gorge, enjoy the lush vegetation and the scenic views, and visit the Rouvas Forest at the end of the trail.

What to Expect: A scenic trail through a lush gorge with diverse flora and fauna. The hike is moderately challenging and offers a peaceful escape into nature.

What to Observe: The lush vegetation, the clear river, and the vibrant birdlife. The trail ends in the beautiful Rouvas Forest, a serene woodland area.

Hiking the Rouvas Gorge Trail was a journey into a lush and vibrant natural landscape. The trail followed the river, offering a peaceful and refreshing atmosphere. The diversity of plant life and the sound of birdsong added to the sense of immersion in nature. Reaching the Rouvas Forest at the end of the trail, I felt a deep sense of tranquility and connection with the natural world. It was a rejuvenating escape from the hustle and bustle of everyday life.

Chapter 7. Cultural Immersion: Traditions, Festivals, and Local Life

Experiencing Cretan Music and Dance

Cretan music and dance are integral parts of the island's rich cultural heritage. They offer a vibrant and expressive way to connect with the island's traditions and the spirit of its people. Experiencing Cretan music and dance will immerse you in the island's soulful rhythms, lively melodies, and captivating performances. Let me guide you through the essence of Cretan music and dance, enriched with personal anecdotes and detailed insights to help you fully appreciate their magic.

Introduction to Cretan Music and Dance

Cretan music is characterized by its unique melodies and rhythms, often played on traditional instruments such as the lyra (a three-stringed bowed instrument), the laouto (a type of lute), and the mandolin. The music is deeply emotional and evocative, reflecting the island's history, landscapes, and the lives of its people.

Cretan dance is equally captivating, with its intricate footwork, dynamic movements, and celebratory spirit. Traditional dances such as the pentozali, syrtos, and sousta are performed at festivals, weddings, and other social gatherings, bringing people together in joyous celebration.

Where to Experience Cretan Music and Dance

1. The Rizitika Songs and Dance Festival

- **Location:** Anogia, Crete
- **Prices:** Free to attend
- **Directions**: Anogeia is located in central Crete, about 36 kilometers from Heraklion. You can drive or take a bus from Heraklion to Anogeia.

What to Do: Attend the annual Rizitika Songs and Dance Festival, where you can experience traditional Cretan music and dance performances. Enjoy the live music, dance along with the locals, and savor traditional Cretan cuisine.

What to Expect: A vibrant festival celebrating the rich musical heritage of Crete. The festival features performances by local musicians and dance groups, showcasing traditional rizitika songs and dances.

What to Observe: The heartfelt performances, the intricate dance steps, and the warm, communal atmosphere.

Attending the Rizitika Songs and Dance Festival in Anogeia was a truly unforgettable experience. The village was alive with music and dance, and the sense of community was palpable. The soulful melodies of the rizitika songs resonated deeply, and I found myself swept up in the joyous energy of the dances. The locals welcomed me with open arms, and I felt a profound connection to the island's cultural heritage.

2. The Kazantzidis Cretan Music and Dance Center

- **Location**: Chania, Crete
- **Prices**: Admission ranges from €10 to €20, depending on the event.
- **Directions**: The center is located in the heart of Chania, easily accessible by foot or taxi from the city center.

What to Do: Attend live music and dance performances, participate in dance workshops, and learn about the history and significance of Cretan music and dance.

What to Expect: A dedicated cultural center offering a variety of events and activities related to Cretan music and dance. The center hosts performances by renowned musicians and dancers, as well as educational workshops.

What to Observe: The skill and passion of the performers, the lively atmosphere, and the opportunity to learn traditional dance steps.

Visiting the Kazantzidis Cretan Music and Dance Center in Chania was an enriching experience. The center's vibrant atmosphere and dedication to preserving Cretan culture were evident in every performance and workshop. Participating in a dance workshop, I learned the intricate steps of the pentozali and syrtos dances. The experience was both challenging and exhilarating, and I left with a newfound appreciation for the skill and artistry of Cretan dance.

3. The Cretan Music and Dance Evenings at Traditional Tavernas

- **Location**: Various traditional tavernas across Crete, including those in Heraklion, Rethymnon, and Chania
- **Prices**: Prices vary depending on the taverna, with an average cost of €20 to €50 per person for dinner and entertainment.
- **Directions**: Traditional tavernas are located in the heart of major cities and picturesque villages. They are easily accessible by foot, taxi, or public transport.

What to Do: Enjoy a delicious meal of traditional Cretan cuisine while being entertained by live music and dance performances. Dance along with the locals and immerse yourself in the festive atmosphere.

What to Expect: An intimate and authentic cultural experience, where you can enjoy the best of Cretan hospitality, music, and dance. The evenings feature performances by local musicians and dancers, creating a lively and joyous ambiance.

What to Observe: The genuine passion and energy of the performers, the warm hospitality of the taverna staff, and the sense of camaraderie among the guests.

One of my most memorable experiences was an evening at a traditional taverna in Rethymnon. The aroma of delicious Cretan dishes filled the air as the musicians began to play their soulful melodies. The dancers, dressed in traditional costumes, captivated us with their graceful and energetic movements. The atmosphere was electric, and I found myself joining in the dances with the locals. The laughter, music, and sense of community made it a night to remember.

Practical Tips for Experiencing Cretan Music and Dance

Timing: Plan your visit around festivals, special events, or evenings when live performances are scheduled at local tavernas. Check event schedules and book tickets in advance if necessary.

Accessibility: Most festivals and performances are accessible by public transport or car. Traditional tavernas are often located in central areas, making them easy to reach.

Participation: Don't be afraid to join in the dances or sing along with the music. The locals will appreciate your enthusiasm and may even teach you a few steps.

Photography: Bring a camera to capture the lively performances, but be mindful of the performers and other guests. Some venues may have restrictions on photography.

Refreshments: Enjoy traditional Cretan dishes and beverages while you immerse yourself in the music and dance. Be sure to try local specialties such as dakos, moussaka, and raki.

Participating in the dances and singing along with the music added a whole new dimension to my experience. The locals were incredibly welcoming and eager to share their culture with me. It was a wonderful way to connect with the people and the island's traditions.

Traditional Festivals and Events

Crete is a land of vibrant traditions and lively festivals that offer a deep dive into the island's rich cultural heritage. Experiencing these events allows you to connect with the local community, enjoy traditional music and dance, and savor the unique flavors of Cretan cuisine. Let me guide you through some of the most significant traditional festivals and events in Crete, enriched with personal anecdotes and detailed insights to help you fully appreciate their charm.

1. Carnival of Rethymnon (Apokries)

- **Location**: Rethymnon, Crete
- **Prices**: Free to attend; costs for food, drinks, and souvenirs vary.
- **Directions**: Rethymnon is located on the northern coast of Crete, easily accessible by car, bus, or taxi from major cities like Heraklion and Chania.

What to Do: Join the colorful parades, participate in street parties, and enjoy live music and dance performances. Indulge in traditional Cretan food and drinks at local tavernas and street vendors.

What to Expect: A lively and extravagant celebration filled with costumes, masks, and elaborate floats. The carnival takes place in the weeks leading up to Lent, culminating in a grand parade.

What to Observe: The creativity and craftsmanship of the costumes and floats, the joyful atmosphere, and the sense of community and tradition.

Attending the Carnival of Rethymnon was an explosion of color and joy. The streets were filled with people in elaborate costumes, dancing and celebrating together. The grand parade was a highlight, with impressive floats and lively music creating an unforgettable spectacle. The sense of camaraderie and the infectious energy made me feel like I was part of something truly special.

2. Easter Celebrations

- **Location**: Throughout Crete, with major celebrations in Heraklion, Chania, and Rethymnon

- **Prices**: Free to attend; costs for food, drinks, and souvenirs vary.
- **Directions**: Major cities like Heraklion, Chania, and Rethymnon are easily accessible by car, bus, or taxi from other parts of Crete.

What to Do: Attend the Holy Week services, participate in the Good Friday processions, and join the midnight Resurrection service on Holy Saturday. Enjoy the traditional Easter feast on Easter Sunday.

What to Expect: A deeply spiritual and festive celebration, with church services, processions, and feasting. The highlight is the midnight Resurrection service, followed by a festive meal with family and friends.

What to Observe: The solemnity of the Good Friday processions, the joy and excitement of the Resurrection service, and the delicious traditional Easter foods such as lamb, koulourakia (Easter cookies), and red-dyed eggs.

Celebrating Easter in Crete was a deeply moving and joyous experience. The Good Friday processions were solemn and reflective, with the entire community coming together to honor the occasion. The midnight Resurrection service was filled with anticipation, and the moment when the church bells rang out, signaling the resurrection of Christ, was truly magical. Sharing the festive Easter meal with new friends and savoring the delicious traditional dishes made the celebration even more special.

3. The Chania Wine Festival

- **Location**: Chania, Crete
- **Prices**: Admission is typically around €10-€20, which includes wine tasting and food samples.
- **Directions**: Chania is located on the northwestern coast of Crete, easily accessible by car, bus, or taxi from other parts of the island.

What to Do: Sample a variety of local wines, enjoy traditional Cretan food, and participate in wine-related activities and workshops. Listen to live music and watch traditional dance performances.

What to Expect: A festive celebration of Cretan wine and gastronomy, with a focus on local vineyards and wineries. The festival features wine tastings, food stalls, and cultural events.

What to Observe: The diverse range of Cretan wines, the culinary delights, and the vibrant cultural performances.

The Chania Wine Festival was a delightful celebration of Cretan wine and food. The opportunity to sample a wide variety of local wines, each with its unique flavor profile, was a highlight. The festival's lively atmosphere was enhanced by traditional music and dance performances, creating a perfect blend of culture and gastronomy. Engaging with local winemakers and learning about their craft added depth to the experience.

4. The Renaissance Festival of Rethymnon

- **Location**: Rethymnon, Crete
- **Prices**: Free to attend; costs for food, drinks, and souvenirs vary.
- **Directions**: Rethymnon is located on the northern coast of Crete, easily accessible by car, bus, or taxi from major cities like Heraklion and Chania.

What to Do: Enjoy theatrical performances, music concerts, and dance shows inspired by the Renaissance period. Explore art exhibitions and attend workshops on traditional crafts.

What to Expect: A cultural festival celebrating the Renaissance heritage of Rethymnon, with a focus on art, music, and theater. The festival takes place in the historic Old Town, adding to the ambiance.

What to Observe: The high-quality performances, the creative art exhibitions, and the historic setting of Rethymnon's Old Town.

The Renaissance Festival of Rethymnon was a journey back in time. The historic Old Town provided the perfect backdrop for the performances and exhibitions, creating an immersive experience. The theatrical performances and music concerts were captivating, and the art exhibitions showcased incredible talent. The festival's blend of history and creativity made it a unique and enriching cultural experience.

Visiting Villages: Anogia, Archanes, and Margarites

Exploring the charming villages of Crete offers an authentic and immersive experience, allowing you to connect with the island's rich cultural heritage and local life. Villages like Anogia, Archanes, and Margarites provide unique opportunities to experience traditional crafts, local cuisine, historic landmarks, and warm hospitality. Let me guide you through these picturesque villages, enriched with personal anecdotes and detailed insights to help you fully appreciate their charm.

1. Anogia: A Village of Tradition and Resilience

- **Location**: Central Crete, in the foothills of Mount Psiloritis
- **Prices**: Free to explore; costs for food, drinks, and souvenirs vary.
- **Directions**: Anogia is about 36 kilometers from Heraklion. You can drive or take a bus from Heraklion to Anogia. The drive takes about 1 hour.

What to Do: Visit the historical sites, explore the local shops and workshops, and enjoy traditional Cretan cuisine at local tavernas. Attend local festivals and events to experience the village's vibrant culture.

What to Expect: A village known for its strong cultural traditions, vibrant music scene, and resilient spirit. Anogia has a rich history and is renowned for its weaving and handicrafts.

What to Observe: The traditional stone houses, the intricate woven textiles and handicrafts, and the lively music and dance performances.

houses and vibrant cultural scene. The local weavers showcased their intricate textiles, each piece telling a story of craftsmanship and heritage. The Memorial of Resistance was a poignant reminder of the village's resilience during World War II. Attending the Rizitika Songs and Dance Festival, I was swept away by the heartfelt performances and the sense of community. Anogeia's rich cultural heritage and warm hospitality made it an unforgettable experience.

2. Archanes: A Village of History and Wine

Visiting Anogia was like stepping into a living museum of Cretan tradition. I was immediately struck by the authenticity of the village, with its traditional stone

- **Location**: Northern Crete, near Heraklion
- **Prices**: Free to explore; costs for food, drinks, and souvenirs vary.

- **Directions**: Archanes is about 16 kilometers south of Heraklion. You can drive or take a bus from Heraklion to Archanes. The drive takes about 30 minutes.

What to Do: Visit the archaeological sites, explore the local wineries, and enjoy traditional Cretan cuisine at local tavernas. Wander through the village's charming streets and admire the well-preserved architecture.

What to Expect: A village with a rich history, known for its archaeological sites and wine production. Archanes is surrounded by vineyards and offers a picturesque setting with traditional stone houses and vibrant gardens.

What to Observe: The archaeological sites, the vineyards and wineries, and the beautifully restored buildings.

Archanes was a delightful blend of history, culture, and natural beauty. The archaeological sites, such as the Minoan Palace of Archanes, provided a fascinating glimpse into the ancient past. Exploring the local wineries was a highlight, as I sampled a variety of exquisite wines and learned about the traditional winemaking process. The village's well-preserved architecture and vibrant gardens added to its charm. Wandering through the streets of Archanes, I felt a deep connection to the island's rich heritage and the timeless beauty of its landscapes.

Visiting villages like Anogeia, Archanes, and Margarites offers an authentic and immersive experience, allowing you to connect with Crete's rich cultural heritage and local life. These villages, each with its unique charm and character, promise unforgettable moments of discovery and connection. My friends, as you explore Crete, make sure to visit these picturesque villages and immerse yourself in their beauty and traditions. May your journey be filled with wonder, joy, and unforgettable memories.

Engaging with Local Artisans and Craftsmen

One of the most enriching ways to immerse yourself in Cretan culture is by engaging with local artisans and craftsmen. These skilled individuals preserve and promote traditional crafts, creating beautiful and unique items that reflect the island's heritage. From pottery and weaving to leatherwork and iconography, each craft tells a story of creativity, tradition, and passion. Let me guide you through some of the best places to engage with local artisans and craftsmen, enriched with personal anecdotes and detailed insights to help you fully appreciate their artistry.

1. Pottery in Margarites

- **Location**: Margarites, central Crete, near Rethymnon
- **Prices**: Free to explore; pottery prices range from €5 to €100 depending on the item.
- **Directions**: Margarites is about 27 kilometers southeast of Rethymnon. You can drive or take a bus from Rethymnon to Margarites. The drive takes about 45 minutes.

What to Do: Visit the pottery workshops, watch demonstrations of traditional pottery techniques, and purchase unique handmade ceramics.

What to Expect: A village renowned for its pottery and craftsmanship. Margarites is home to numerous pottery workshops where you can see artisans at work and purchase beautifully crafted items.

What to Observe: The intricate designs and vibrant colors of the pottery, the skill and dedication of the artisans, and the opportunity to participate in pottery-making workshops.

Visiting the pottery workshops in Margarites was an enlightening experience. I watched the skilled potters as they transformed clay into beautiful and functional works of art. The intricate designs and vibrant colors of the ceramics were captivating. One potter invited me to try my hand at shaping clay on the potter's wheel, and the experience was both challenging and rewarding. Purchasing a handmade vase as a souvenir, I left with a deeper appreciation for the craftsmanship and creativity of the local artisans.

2. Weaving in Anogeia

- **Location**: Anogeia, central Crete, in the foothills of Mount Psiloritis
- **Prices**: Free to explore; woven textiles range from €10 to €200 depending on the item.
- **Directions**: Anogeia is about 36 kilometers from Heraklion. You can drive or take a bus from Heraklion to Anogeia. The drive takes about 1 hour.

What to Do: Visit the weaving workshops, watch demonstrations of traditional weaving techniques, and purchase intricately woven textiles.

What to Expect: A village known for its strong cultural traditions and vibrant weaving scene. Anogeia is home to several weaving workshops where you can see artisans at work and purchase beautifully crafted textiles.

What to Observe: The intricate patterns and vibrant colors of the woven textiles, the skill and dedication of the weavers, and the opportunity to participate in weaving workshops.

The weaving workshops in Anogeia were a highlight of my visit. Watching the skilled weavers create intricate patterns on their looms was mesmerizing. The vibrant colors and detailed designs of the textiles were a testament to their craftsmanship. One weaver invited me to try weaving on a traditional loom, and the experience was both challenging and rewarding. I purchased a beautifully woven scarf as a keepsake, leaving with a deeper appreciation for the artistry and tradition of Cretan weaving.

3. Leatherwork in Chania

- **Location**: Chania, northwestern Crete
- **Prices**: Free to explore; leather goods range from €20 to €200 depending on the item.
- **Directions**: Chania is located on the northwestern coast of Crete. The leather workshops are situated

in the Old Town, easily accessible by foot, taxi, or public transport.

What to Do: Visit the leather workshops, watch demonstrations of traditional leatherworking techniques, and purchase high-quality leather goods.

What to Expect: Chania is known for its leather goods, and the Old Town is home to numerous leather workshops where you can see artisans at work and purchase beautifully crafted items.

What to Observe: The intricate designs and high-quality craftsmanship of the leather goods, the skill and dedication of the leatherworkers, and the opportunity to participate in leatherworking workshops.

Exploring the leather workshops in Chania's Old Town was a fascinating experience. The smell of leather and the sight of skilled craftsmen creating beautiful bags, belts, and sandals added to the charm of the experience. One leatherworker invited me to observe the detailed process of hand-stitching a leather bag. The attention to detail and dedication to quality were evident in every stitch. I purchased a handcrafted leather wallet as a memento, leaving with a deeper appreciation for the craftsmanship and tradition of Cretan leatherwork.

3. Iconography in Heraklion

- **Location**: Heraklion, northern Crete
- **Prices**: Free to explore; icons range from €50 to €500 depending on the item.
- **Directions**: Heraklion is located on the northern coast of Crete. The

iconography workshops are situated in the city center, easily accessible by foot, taxi, or public transport.

What to Do: Visit the iconography workshops, watch demonstrations of traditional icon-painting techniques, and purchase beautifully crafted icons.

What to Expect: Heraklion is known for its religious iconography, and the city center is home to several workshops where you can see artisans at work and purchase hand-painted icons.

What to Observe: The intricate designs and vibrant colors of the icons, the skill and dedication of the iconographers, and the opportunity to learn about the history and significance of religious iconography.

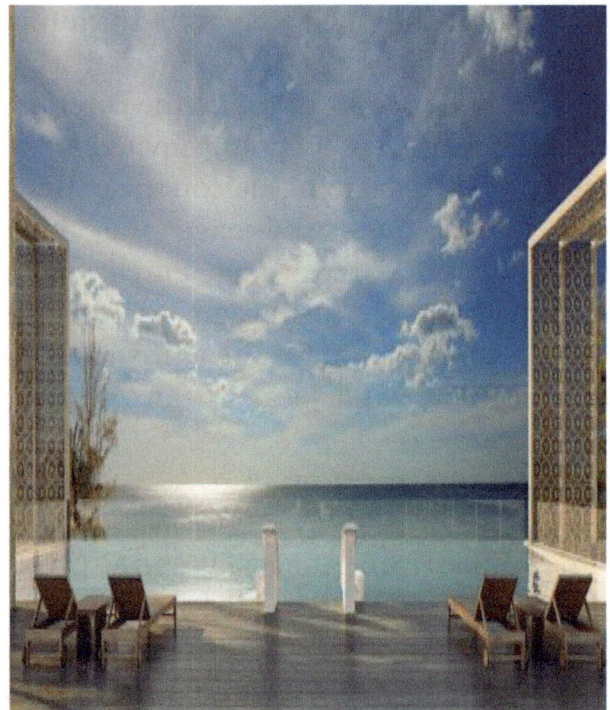

Visiting the iconography workshops in Heraklion was a deeply enriching experience. The skill and devotion of the iconographers were evident in their intricate and beautiful creations. One iconographer invited me to observe the meticulous process of painting an icon, explaining the significance of each detail. The patience and precision required to create these works of art were truly impressive. I purchased a hand-painted icon as a meaningful souvenir, leaving with a deeper appreciation for the artistry and spiritual significance of Cretan iconography.

Practical Tips for Engaging with Local Artisans

Timing: Visit workshops and galleries during their opening hours, typically in the morning and late afternoon. Weekdays are generally quieter, allowing for a more intimate experience.

Accessibility: Most workshops are accessible by car or public transport. Wear comfortable shoes for walking and exploring.

Participation: Engage with the artisans, ask questions, and express your interest in their craft. Many workshops offer hands-on experiences and demonstrations, so don't hesitate to participate.

Photography: Bring a camera to capture the intricate details of the crafts, but be respectful of the artisans and ask for permission before taking photos.

Refreshments: Enjoy traditional Cretan food and drinks at local tavernas. Be sure to try local specialties and support family-owned businesses.

Engaging with the local artisans and participating in their workshops added a whole new dimension to my experience. The warmth and hospitality of the Cretan people made me feel welcome and included, and I learned so much about their traditions and way of life. Purchasing handmade items as souvenirs created lasting memories of connection and joy.

Engaging with local artisans and craftsmen in Crete offers an authentic and immersive experience, allowing you to connect with the island's rich cultural heritage and creative spirit. From pottery and weaving to leatherwork and iconography, these artisans preserve and promote traditional crafts, creating beautiful and unique items that reflect the island's heritage. My friends, as you explore Crete, make sure to visit these talented artisans and immerse yourself in their artistry and passion. May your journey be filled with wonder, creativity, and unforgettable memories.

Chapter 8. Adventure and Outdoor Activities

Water Sports: Diving, Snorkeling, and Sailing

Crete's stunning coastline and crystal-clear waters make it a paradise for water sports enthusiasts. Whether you're an experienced diver, a snorkeling novice, or a sailing aficionado, the island offers a wealth of opportunities to explore its marine beauty and embrace the thrill of the open sea. Let me guide you through the best spots and experiences for diving, snorkeling, and sailing in Crete, enriched with personal anecdotes and detailed insights to help you make the most of your aquatic adventures.

Top Diving Spots

1. Elounda Bay

- **Location**: Northeastern Crete, near Agios Nikolaos
- **Prices**: Dive packages range from €50 to €100, depending on the number of dives and equipment rental.
- **Directions**: Drive or take a bus to Elounda from Agios Nikolaos,

approximately 10 kilometers away. The drive takes about 20 minutes.

What to Do: Explore underwater caves, reefs, and shipwrecks. Participate in guided dives with local dive centers.

What to Expect: A diverse underwater landscape with crystal-clear waters, vibrant marine life, and fascinating shipwrecks.

What to Observe: The colorful coral reefs, schools of fish, and the remnants of ancient shipwrecks.

Diving in Elounda Bay was an unforgettable experience. The crystal-clear waters provided perfect visibility, allowing me to fully appreciate the vibrant coral reefs and marine life. Exploring the underwater caves and discovering a centuries-old shipwreck added an element of adventure and mystery to the dive. The local dive center provided excellent guidance and equipment, making the experience both safe and exhilarating.

2. Chania

- **Location**: Northwestern Crete
- **Prices**: Dive packages range from €50 to €100, depending on the number of dives and equipment rental.
- **Directions**: Drive or take a bus to Chania from other parts of the island. The city is well-connected by public transport.

What to Do: Dive sites include Elephant Cave, with its impressive stalactites and stalagmites, and the HMS Perseus wreck.

What to Expect: A variety of dive sites offering unique underwater landscapes and historical shipwrecks.

What to Observe: The intricate rock formations, the colorful marine life, and the remains of historical wrecks.

Diving in Chania was a mesmerizing journey into the depths of the sea. The Elephant Cave, with its stunning stalactites and stalagmites, was a surreal underwater wonderland. The highlight of the dive was exploring the HMS Perseus wreck, a World War II submarine that now serves as an artificial reef teeming with marine life. The sense of history and the vibrant underwater scenery made the dive an unforgettable experience.

Top Snorkeling Spots

1. Balos Lagoon

- **Location**: Northwestern Crete, near Kissamos
- **Prices**: Free to snorkel; equipment rental ranges from €10 to €20.
- **Directions**: Drive to Kissamos and take a boat to Balos Lagoon, or hike from Kaliviani. The boat ride takes about an hour, while the hike offers stunning views along the way.

What to Do: Snorkel in the shallow, turquoise waters of the lagoon, exploring the vibrant marine life and the sandy seabed.

What to Expect: Crystal-clear waters, shallow lagoons, and a diverse array of marine life, including colorful fish and sea urchins.

What to Observe: The vibrant marine life, the clear turquoise waters, and the beautiful sandy seabed.

Snorkeling in Balos Lagoon was like swimming in a giant natural aquarium. The clear turquoise waters provided perfect visibility, allowing me to observe the colorful fish and sea urchins up close. The sandy seabed and the gentle waves created a serene and relaxing environment. The stunning scenery above and below the water made it a truly magical experience.

2. Elafonissi Beach

- **Location**: Southwestern Crete
- **Prices**: Free to snorkel; equipment rental ranges from €10 to €20.
- **Directions**: Drive or take a bus to Elafonissi from Chania, approximately 76 kilometers away. The drive takes about 1.5 to 2 hours.

What to Do: Snorkel in the shallow lagoons and explore the underwater rock formations and coral reefs.

What to Expect: Shallow, warm waters with excellent visibility and diverse marine life.

What to Observe: The colorful coral reefs, the schools of fish, and the intricate rock formations.

Snorkeling at Elafonissi Beach was an enchanting experience. The shallow lagoons with their warm, clear waters were perfect for observing the vibrant marine life. The coral reefs and underwater rock formations added an element of intrigue and beauty to the snorkel. The sight of colorful fish darting among the corals was mesmerizing, and I spent hours exploring the underwater world.

Top Sailing Experiences

1. Sailing Around Spinalonga Island

- **Location**: Northeastern Crete, near Elounda and Agios Nikolaos
- **Prices**: Sailing tours range from €50 to €100 per person, depending on the duration and inclusions.
- **Directions**: Drive or take a bus to Elounda or Agios Nikolaos, where sailing tours depart.

What to Do: Sail around Spinalonga Island, enjoy the stunning coastal views, and stop for a swim in the clear waters.

What to Expect: A scenic sailing tour with beautiful coastal landscapes, historical sites, and opportunities for swimming and snorkeling.

What to Observe: The impressive Venetian fortress on Spinalonga Island, the crystal-clear waters, and the diverse marine life.

Sailing around Spinalonga Island was a delightful adventure. The gentle sea breeze and the stunning coastal views created a sense of freedom and tranquility. The highlight of the tour was exploring the Venetian fortress on Spinalonga Island, which offered a fascinating glimpse into the island's history. Stopping for a swim in the clear waters was refreshing, and the diverse marine life added to the enjoyment of the experience.

2. Sunset Sailing Tour in Chania

- **Location**: Chania, northwestern Crete
- **Prices**: Sunset sailing tours range from €40 to €80 per person, depending on the duration and inclusions.
- **Directions**: Drive or take a bus to Chania, where sunset sailing tours depart from the Old Harbor.

What to Do: Enjoy a sunset sailing tour along the coast of Chania, with breathtaking views of the sunset over the Aegean Sea.

What to Expect: A relaxing and scenic sailing tour with stunning sunset views, gentle sea breeze, and opportunities for swimming and snorkeling.

What to Observe: The vibrant colors of the sunset, the scenic coastal landscapes, and the peaceful ambiance of the Aegean Sea.

The sunset sailing tour in Chania was a truly magical experience. As the sun began to set, the sky transformed into a canvas of vibrant colors, casting a golden glow over the Aegean Sea. The gentle sea breeze and the sound of the waves created a serene and peaceful atmosphere. Watching the sunset from the deck of the sailboat was a moment of pure bliss, and it felt like time stood still. The opportunity to swim in the clear waters and snorkel added to the enjoyment of the tour.

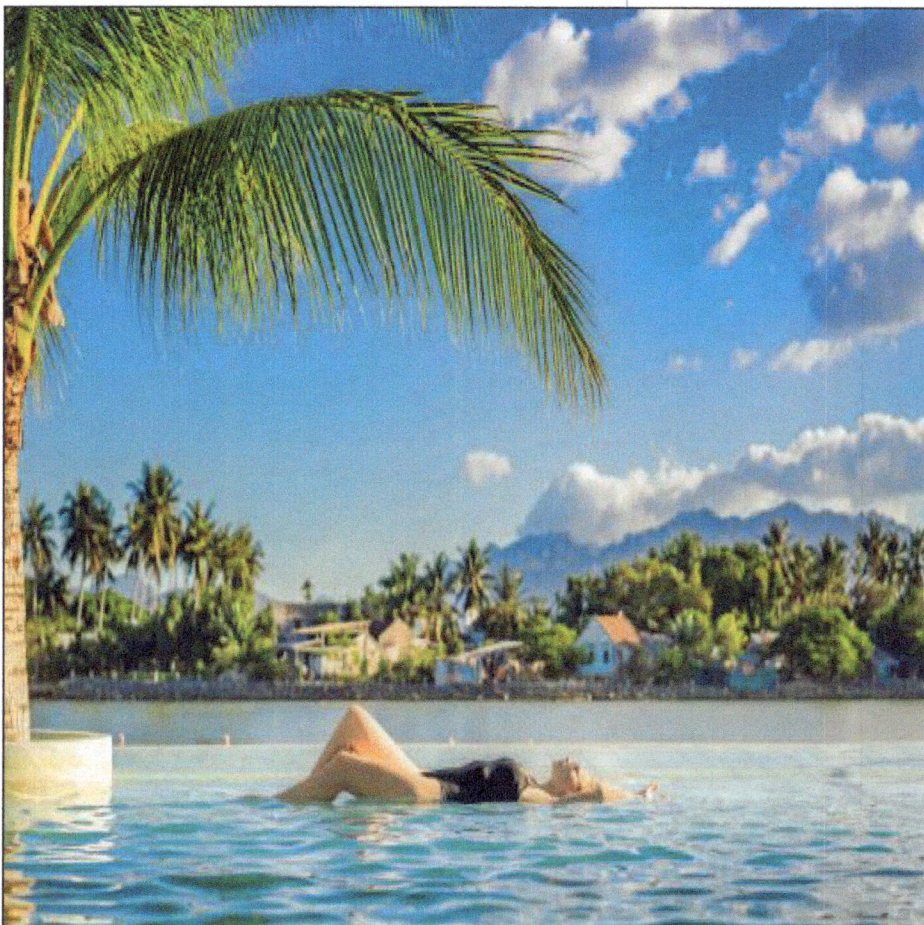

Practical Tips for Water Sports

Timing: The best time for water sports in Crete is during the summer months (June to September) when the weather is warm and the sea conditions are favorable.

Accessibility: Most water sports activities are accessible by car or public transport. Be sure to check the availability of equipment rental and guided tours in advance.

Participation: Whether you're a beginner or an experienced enthusiast, there are options for all skill levels. Local instructors and guides are available to provide training and support.

Safety: Always prioritize safety by following guidelines and instructions from certified instructors and guides. Wear appropriate gear, such as life jackets and wetsuits, and be mindful of the weather and sea conditions.

Photography: Bring a waterproof camera or a GoPro to capture your underwater adventures and scenic sailing tours. Be sure to protect your equipment from water and sand.

Refreshments: Stay hydrated and bring snacks to keep your energy levels up during your activities. Many guided tours also offer refreshments as part of the package.

Staying hydrated and taking breaks between activities ensured that I had the energy and stamina to fully enjoy my water sports adventures. The guidance and support from local instructors and guides made the experiences safe and enjoyable. Capturing the stunning underwater scenes and the scenic sailing tours with my waterproof camera created lasting memories of my time in Crete.

Chapter 9: . Practical Wisdom

Packing List

Packing thoughtfully for your trip to Crete is crucial for ensuring a comfortable, enjoyable, and stress-free experience. By bringing the right items, you'll be prepared for the island's diverse activities, ranging from beach days and hiking adventures to exploring ancient ruins and savoring local cuisine. Here's an extensive, yet concise, packing list designed to cover all the essentials and enhance your journey.

1. Clothing

- **Lightweight Clothing:** Pack breathable, lightweight clothes for the warm Mediterranean climate. Think cotton t-shirts, linen shorts, and sundresses. Price: Prices vary; budget-friendly options available at local stores or online.
- **Layers**: Include a light jacket or sweater for cooler evenings, especially in the mountains. Price: Approximately €20-€50 for a good quality layer.
- **Swimwear**: Bring multiple swimsuits for beach and pool days. Price: €10-€30 each.
- **Hiking Gear:** Comfortable hiking pants, moisture-wicking shirts, and a hat. Price: €30-€100 for quality gear.

I packed a mix of lightweight clothes and layers, and it made a huge difference. The evenings in the mountains could get surprisingly cool, and having a light jacket meant I could enjoy the stunning sunsets without feeling chilly.

2. Footwear

- **Comfortable Walking Shoes**: Essential for exploring historical sites and walking through villages. Price: €50-€100 for quality shoes.
- **Hiking Boots:** For more demanding trails and mountain adventures. Price: €70-€150.

- **Sandals**: Comfortable sandals for beach days and casual outings. Price: €20-€50.

My comfortable walking shoes were a lifesaver when exploring the archaeological sites. Hiking boots were indispensable for trekking through the gorges, and sandals were perfect for relaxing beach days.

3. Accessories

- **Sunglasses**: Protect your eyes from the strong Mediterranean sun. Price: €15-€50.
- **Hat**: A wide-brimmed hat for sun protection. Price: €10-€30.
- **Reusable Water Bottle**: Stay hydrated during your adventures. Price: €10-€20.
- **Daypack**: A small backpack for carrying essentials during day trips. Price: €20-€50.

My wide-brimmed hat and sunglasses were essential for exploring Crete under the sun. The reusable water bottle kept me hydrated, especially during long hikes, and the daypack was perfect for carrying snacks and a camera.

4. Toiletries and Health

- **Sunscreen**: High SPF to protect your skin. Price: €10-€20.
- **Insect Repellent**: To ward off mosquitoes and other insects. Price: €5-€10.
- **First Aid Kit**: Include bandages, antiseptic wipes, and any personal medications. Price: €10-€20.

- **Hand Sanitizer**: Essential for keeping your hands clean. Price: €3-€5.

Sunscreen and insect repellent were non-negotiables for me. They kept my skin protected and comfortable throughout the trip. The first aid kit came in handy more than once, especially during hikes.

5. Technology and Gadgets

- **Camera**: Capture the breathtaking landscapes and memorable moments. Price: Varies; budget-friendly options available.
- **Power Bank**: Keep your devices charged on the go. Price: €20-€40.
- **Adapters and Chargers:** Ensure you can charge your devices with the correct adapters. Price: €10-€20.
- **Smartphone**: For navigation, photos, and staying connected. Price: Varies.

My camera captured stunning photos of the landscapes and historical sites. The power bank was a lifesaver during long day trips, ensuring my smartphone was always charged for navigation and taking pictures.

6. Miscellaneous

- **Travel Guide:** A comprehensive travel guide for Crete. Price: €10-€20.
- **Travel Insurance**: Protect yourself from unexpected events. Price: Varies; typically €30-€100.

- **Snacks**: Bring your favorite snacks for hikes and day trips. Price: Varies.
- **Notebook and Pen**: For jotting down memories and travel tips. Price: €5-€10.

My travel guide provided valuable insights and hidden gems that I wouldn't have discovered otherwise. Travel insurance gave me peace of mind, and having snacks and a notebook on hand added comfort and joy to my travels.

Safety Tips

Why Safety Matters

Your safety is paramount when traveling, and by being prepared, you can ensure a smooth and enjoyable experience. Crete is a beautiful and welcoming island, but like any destination, it has its unique challenges. Being aware of these and taking simple precautions will enhance your journey and allow you to focus on making unforgettable memories.

Health and Medical Tips

1. Stay Hydrated

- **Location**: Throughout Crete
- **Prices**: Bottled water ranges from €0.50 to €1 per liter.
- **Directions**: Purchase bottled water at local supermarkets, kiosks, and cafes.

What to Do: Drink plenty of water, especially in the hot summer months, to avoid dehydration.

What to Expect: The Mediterranean climate can be hot and dry, so it's crucial to stay hydrated.

What to Observe: Signs of dehydration include dizziness, dry mouth, and fatigue.

During my first summer in Crete, I underestimated the heat and found myself feeling dizzy and fatigued. After realizing I hadn't been drinking enough water, I made sure to carry a reusable water bottle everywhere. Staying hydrated made a noticeable difference in my energy levels and overall well-being.

2. Know the Location of Medical Facilities

- **Location**: Major cities like Heraklion, Chania, and Rethymnon
- **Prices**: Free public healthcare for emergencies; private clinics may charge varying fees.
- **Directions**: Locate the nearest hospital or clinic upon arrival. Use maps or ask locals for directions.

What to Do: Familiarize yourself with the location of the nearest medical facilities in case of emergencies.

What to Expect: Both public hospitals and private clinics are available, with English-speaking staff in major cities.

What to Observe: Look for signs indicating hospitals or clinics, and note their operating hours.

On one trip, a friend had a minor accident. Knowing the location of the nearest clinic meant we could get help quickly. The staff were professional and efficient, and being prepared helped minimize stress in an unexpected situation.

Safety on the Road

1. Drive Safely and Responsibly

- **Location**: Throughout Crete
- **Prices**: Car rentals range from €20 to €50 per day, depending on the vehicle.
- **Directions**: Rent a car from reputable agencies in major cities and airports.

What to Do: Follow local traffic laws, wear seat belts, and drive defensively. Be cautious on narrow and winding mountain roads.

What to Expect: Crete's roads can be challenging, with sharp turns and steep inclines. Local driving habits may differ from what you're used to.

What to Observe: Watch out for motorbikes, pedestrians, and livestock on rural roads.

Renting a car allowed me to explore Crete's hidden gems, but driving required extra caution. The mountain roads were narrow and winding, and I often encountered goats crossing the road. Taking my time and driving defensively ensured a safe and enjoyable journey.

2. Use Reputable Taxi Services

- **Location**: Major cities and tourist areas
- **Prices**: Taxi fares vary; typical short trips range from €5 to €15.

- **Directions**: Use licensed taxi services, which can be hailed on the street or booked through apps.

What to Do: Ensure the taxi is licensed, and agree on the fare before starting the trip. Use taxi apps for added security.

What to Expect: Taxis are widely available in cities and tourist areas. Licensed taxis display a meter and the driver's identification.

What to Observe: Look for the taxi's official markings and meter to ensure it's a legitimate service.

Using licensed taxi services gave me peace of mind when traveling in cities. I always confirmed the fare before starting the trip, and using taxi apps added an extra layer of security, especially when traveling at night.

Outdoor and Adventure Safety

1. Follow Hiking and Climbing Guidelines

- **Location**: Hiking trails and climbing spots like Samaria Gorge, Mount Ida, and Agiofarago Gorge
- **Prices**: Entrance fees range from free to €6, depending on the location.
- **Directions**: Access trails from designated entrances, with maps and information available at visitor centers.

What to Do: Stay on marked trails, wear appropriate gear, and check weather conditions before setting out.

What to Expect: Trails and climbing spots can be challenging, with varying levels of difficulty and terrain.

What to Observe: Look for trail markers, warning signs, and information boards. Be aware of potential hazards like loose rocks and steep drops.

Hiking the Samaria Gorge was an incredible experience, but staying on the marked trail was essential for safety. The terrain was rocky and uneven, and wearing sturdy hiking boots made a big difference. Checking the weather forecast and starting early in the morning helped me avoid the midday heat and made the hike more enjoyable.

2. Water Safety at Beaches and Lakes

- **Location**: Popular beaches like Elafonissi, Balos, and Vai, as well as lakes like Kournas
- **Prices**: Free to access; rental fees for water sports equipment vary.
- **Directions**: Access beaches and lakes from designated parking areas or public transport stops.

What to Do: Swim in designated areas, follow lifeguard instructions, and be aware of currents and tides.

What to Expect: Beaches and lakes can have strong currents, varying depths, and underwater hazards.

What to Observe: Look for warning flags, signs, and lifeguards on duty. Be cautious of sudden drops and underwater rocks.

Swimming at Elafonissi Beach was a highlight of my trip, but I made sure to stay within the designated swimming areas. The clear water can be deceptively deep in some spots, and being aware of the currents kept me safe. Observing the warning flags and lifeguard instructions added an extra layer of security.

General Safety Tips

1. Be Aware of Your Surroundings

- **Location**: Throughout Crete
- **Prices**: Free
- **Directions**: Stay vigilant in crowded areas like markets, tourist attractions, and public transport.

What to Do: Keep an eye on your belongings, avoid displaying valuable items, and stay aware of your surroundings.

What to Expect: Crowded areas can attract pickpockets and petty thieves.

What to Observe: Be mindful of your personal space and belongings, and trust your instincts if something feels off.

Exploring the bustling markets of Heraklion was an exciting experience, but it was important to stay aware of my surroundings. Keeping my belongings secure and being mindful of my personal space helped me avoid any potential issues and allowed me to enjoy the vibrant atmosphere.

2. Respect Local Customs and Traditions

- **Location**: Throughout Crete
- **Prices**: Free
- **Directions**: Learn about local customs and traditions before your trip, and observe them during your stay.

What to Do: Dress modestly when visiting religious sites, ask for permission before taking photos of people, and be courteous and respectful.

What to Expect: Crete has a rich cultural heritage, and respecting local customs enhances your experience and fosters positive interactions.

What to Observe: Notice how locals behave and follow their lead, especially in places of worship and during festivals.

Respecting local customs enriched my experience in Crete. When visiting monasteries and churches, dressing modestly and observing the etiquette allowed me to connect with the local culture. Asking for permission before taking photos of people and being courteous opened doors to meaningful interactions and friendships.

Resources: Emergency Contacts, Medical Centers, and Apps for Real-Time Updates

Practical Wisdom: Resources for Safety and Convenience

Why These Resources are Essential

Having access to reliable resources such as emergency contacts, medical centers, and apps for real-time updates is crucial for ensuring a safe and stress-free trip. By being prepared and knowing where to turn for help, you can enjoy your journey with peace of mind, knowing you're equipped to handle any situation that arises. Here's a detailed guide to essential resources for your adventure in Crete.

Emergency Contacts

Key Contacts

1. Emergency Services (Police, Fire, Ambulance):
- **Phone Number**: 112
- **Location**: Available throughout Crete
- **Price**: Free
- **Directions**: Dial 112 from any phone for immediate assistance.

What to Do: Provide your location and details of the emergency.

What to Expect: Prompt response from the nearest emergency services.

What to Observe: Emergency responders in uniform; may arrive with marked vehicles.

Knowing that 112 is the universal emergency number in Crete gave me peace of mind throughout my travels. Thankfully, I never had to use it, but having it saved in my phone was a reassuring step that made me feel prepared for any unexpected situations.

2. Tourist Police:

- **Phone Number**: 171
- **Location:** Major tourist areas such as Heraklion, Chania, and Rethymnon
- **Price**: Free
- **Directions**: Dial 171 for assistance with tourist-related issues.
- **What to Do:** Explain your situation to the operator, who can provide guidance and support.
- **What to Expect**: Assistance with issues such as lost documents, theft, or safety concerns.
- **What to Observe**: Officers in uniform, often multilingual.

When a fellow traveler misplaced their passport, the Tourist Police were incredibly helpful in guiding them through the process of reporting the loss and obtaining a temporary travel document. Their efficiency and support made a stressful situation much more manageable.

Medical Centers

Key Medical Facilities

1. University Hospital of Heraklion:

- **Location**: Stavrakia, Heraklion
- **Prices**: Public healthcare is free for emergencies; fees apply for other services.
- **Directions**: Drive or take a bus to the hospital from Heraklion city center.

What to Do: Go to the emergency department for urgent medical care.

What to Expect: Professional medical services with English-speaking staff available.

What to Observe: Modern medical facilities and equipment; signs directing you to various departments.

During my stay in Crete, a friend needed medical attention for a minor injury. The staff at the University Hospital of Heraklion were attentive and professional, providing excellent care and explaining everything in English, which made the experience reassuring and smooth.

2. Chania General Hospital:

- **Location**: Mournies, Chania
- **Prices**: Public healthcare is free for emergencies; fees apply for other services.
- **Directions**: Drive or take a bus to the hospital from Chania city center.

What to Do: Go to the emergency department for urgent medical care.

What to Expect: High-quality medical services with multilingual staff available.

What to Observe: Clean and well-maintained facilities; clear signage for different departments.

Knowing the location and quality of the Chania General Hospital added an extra layer of confidence during my trip. While I didn't need to visit, being aware of this resource was comforting and allowed me to enjoy my adventures without worry.

Apps for Real-Time Updates

Essential Apps

1. Greek Travel Guide App:

- **Price**: Free
- **Download**: Available on iOS and Android

What to Do: Use the app for real-time updates on travel advisories, weather conditions, and local events.

What to Expect: Comprehensive and up-to-date information to enhance your travel experience.

What to Observe: User-friendly interface with features such as offline maps, language translation, and emergency contact information.

The Greek Travel Guide App became my go-to resource for real-time updates. Whether checking the weather before a hike or finding local events, the app's comprehensive information and offline maps were invaluable. It even helped me navigate language barriers with its translation feature.

2. WhatsApp:

- **Price**: Free
- **Download**: Available on iOS and Android

What to Do: Use WhatsApp for communication with friends, family, and local contacts. Join group chats for real-time updates on travel plans and safety alerts.

What to Expect: Reliable messaging and calling service with end-to-end encryption for privacy.

What to Observe: Quick and easy communication; ability to share location and multimedia files.

WhatsApp was essential for staying connected with fellow travelers and local guides. Its group chat feature allowed us to share updates and changes in plans instantly, ensuring everyone was informed and safe. The ability to share my location with friends and family added an extra layer of security and comfort.

3. Google Maps:
- **Price**: Free
- **Download**: Available on iOS and Android

What to Do: Use Google Maps for navigation, finding local attractions, and real-time traffic updates.

What to Expect: Accurate and reliable maps with features such as offline navigation, public transport information, and street view.

What to Observe: Detailed maps, easy-to-follow directions, and real-time updates on traffic conditions.

Google Maps was a lifesaver during my travels in Crete. Whether navigating through winding mountain roads or finding a hidden beach, the app's accurate directions and real-time traffic updates made every journey smooth and stress-free. The offline maps feature was particularly useful in remote areas with limited connectivity.

Chapter 10: Conclusion

Final Thoughts

mountains and lush valleys, the island's natural beauty is breathtaking. The historical landmarks and archeological riches are intriguing glimpses into the past, while the bustling festivals and customs give a vivid and immersive cultural experience.

Location: Crete, Greece. Prices vary based on activities and lodgings.
Directions: Accessible by plane via Heraklion and Chania airports or by boat from the mainland Greece
Explore beaches such as Elafonissi and Balos, walk the Samaria Gorge, see the Palace of Knossos, and attend local festivals.
What to expect: A varied and intriguing location with a rich cultural history and stunning scenery.
What to See: The contrasts between busy cities and peaceful villages, the brilliant hues of the natural surroundings, and the friendly residents.

As you prepare to go on your vacation to the wonderful island of Crete, I hope this book has given you the insights and knowledge you need to make your trip really memorable. Crete is a place of breathtaking scenery, rich history, lively culture, and genuine hospitality. Every time spent on this wonderful island will leave you with fond memories and a greater appreciation for its distinct charm.

Enjoy the beauty and diversity of Crete.

Crete is a location that has something for everyone. From the sun-kissed beaches and crystal-clear oceans to the towering

My tour across Crete was a tapestry of amazing moments. Every moment was full of amazement and discovery, from the tranquility of Elafonissi Beach with its pink-hued beaches to the thrilling climb through the Samaria Gorge. Visiting the Palace of Knossos felt like going back in time, and the vibrant festivals brought the island's traditions to life. The Cretan people's real warmth and kindness made me feel like at home, and I departed with a strong connection to this lovely island.

Practical tips for a seamless experience

To ensure your travel is seamless and pleasurable, keep these crucial guidelines in mind:

1. Plan ahead and be informed.

Location: Throughout Crete.
Directions: Use travel guides, internet, and apps to plan and keep informed. Prices: Free.
What to Do: Research your travels, check weather predictions, and get acquainted with local traditions.
What To Expect: A well-planned journey helps you to maximize your time while avoiding unforeseen shocks.
What to Look for: Changes in the weather, local events, and any travel warnings.

My vacation to Crete was stress-free and pleasurable thanks to careful planning. Checking weather predictions helped me prepare wisely, and knowing local traditions improved my cultural experience. Staying updated about local events guaranteed that I did not miss out on any memorable celebrations.

2. Stay safe and prepared.

Location: Throughout Crete.
Directions: Keep emergency contacts and medical information ready, and download necessary travel applications. Prices: Free.
What to Do: Stay hydrated, utilize trustworthy transportation providers, and adhere to outdoor safety requirements.
What To Expect: A secure and stress-free environment where you can completely enjoy your experiences.
What to Look Out For: Dehydration signs, road conditions, and activity safety cautions.

Staying safe and prepared was essential for a worry-free vacation. Knowing the whereabouts of medical facilities and having emergency contacts stored on my phone gave me peace of mind. Using travel applications kept me informed and connected, resulting in a seamless and delightful trip.

3. Embrace Local Culture.

Location: Throughout Crete.
Prices: vary according on activity.
Directions: Interact with the people, attend festivals, and explore cultural places.
What to do: Take part in traditional dances, enjoy local food, and learn about Cretan history and customs.

What to Expect: An enriching and engaging cultural experience that strengthens your relationship to Crete.

What to Look for: The real warmth and welcome of people, the brilliant colors and sounds of festivals, and the fine features of historical landmarks.

Embracing local culture was the highlight of my journey. Dancing at a traditional festival, eating great Cretan cuisine, and learning about the island's history from locals all enhanced my trip and left me with a deep respect for Crete's distinct heritage.

Last Note For Your Journey

Crete is a paradise that captures both the heart and spirit. Its natural beauty, rich history, lively culture, and kind hospitality weave a tapestry of memories that will remain with you long after your trip is over. As you begin on your journey to this wonderful island, remember to live each moment with an open heart and a feeling of awe. May your journeys be full with adventure, discovery, and wonderful experiences.

Price Ranges: Accommodations, activities, and eating choices vary greatly, enabling you to adapt your vacation to your own budget and tastes.

Directions: Crete is readily accessible by air and boat, with several transit alternatives for touring the island.

What to Do: Immerse yourself in the island's beauty, history, and culture by partaking in a variety of activities.

What to Expect: A tour that provides the ideal balance of leisure, adventure, and cultural enrichment.

What to See: The ever-changing scenery, lively local customs, and the real kindness of the Cretans.

As I think on my travels around Crete, I'm grateful for the memorable experiences and contacts I had. The island's beauty, culture, and people have made an unforgettable impression on my heart. I hope your trip in Crete is as lovely and enriching as mine was.

Tips For Returning Home

As your stay in Crete draws to a conclusion, you'll need to plan your return trip carefully. Reflecting on your experiences and taking precautions to guarantee a seamless transition might help you retain the beauty of your trips while readjusting to your normal life with ease. Here are some crucial recommendations for going home, along with personal experiences and in-depth views.

- **Collect and preserve memories**.

Location: Throughout Crete.
Prices: Free to collect; the price of souvenirs varies.
Directions: Look for unusual products at local markets, boutiques, and galleries.

What to Do: Keep a vacation notebook to record memories, snap photos, and collect keepsakes.

What to Expect: An extensive collection of memories and souvenirs that reflect the soul of your vacation.

What to Look for: The exceptional workmanship of local artists, the beauty of the landscapes, and the experiences that made your trip memorable.

During my journey to Crete, I acquired modest souvenirs such as handmade ceramics, native spices, and stunning images. Writing in my trip notebook every evening allowed me to record the feelings and events of the day. These experiences and artifacts become treasured keepsakes from my fantastic adventure.

- **Plan Your Journey Back Home**

Location: Airports and ports in Heraklion and Chania.

Prices vary based on transportation and services.

Directions: Book your transportation ahead of time and, if feasible, check in online.

What to Do: Confirm your trip plans, arrive to the airport or port early, and prepare all relevant paperwork.

What to Expect: A more stress-free travel experience with fewer last-minute surprises.

What to Look for: Departure timings, gate information, and any updates or modifications to your trip itinerary.

Making sure all of my travel plans were finalized in advance helped the departing process go smoothly. Arriving at the airport early helped me to unwind and think on my journey as I waited for my flight. All of my paperwork were organized and readily accessible, which made check-in and security go more smoothly.

- **Manage your finances**.

Location: Banks and ATMs all across Crete.

Prices vary based on transactions and services.

Directions: If necessary, withdraw cash and pay any outstanding debts before departing.

What to do: Exchange any leftover cash, pay any overdue debts, and retain all receipts for your records.

What to Expect: A smooth transfer with financial issues in order.

What to look for: Exchange rates, transaction fees, and the presence of ATMs and banks.

Before departing Crete, I went to a local bank to convert my remaining euros and pay any outstanding debts. This meant that I didn't have any unresolved money issues when I returned home. Keeping receipts and a record of my costs allowed me to manage my budget and reflect on my spending on the trip.

Made in United States
North Haven, CT
17 June 2025